PANPSYCHISM
AND THE
COMBINATION
PROBLEM

Panpsychism and the Combination Problem

Santtu Heikkinen

Creative Fire Press
- 2021 -

CREATIVE FIRE PRESS

This edition copyright © 2021, by Santtu Heikkinen

Edited by David Skrbina

All rights reserved. No part of this publication may be reproduced, stored in a retrieval system, or transmitted, in any form or by any means, electronic, mechanical, photocopying, recording, or otherwise.

Creative Fire Press is a division of The Walden Group, a Michigan non-profit educational corporation.

Library of Congress Cataloging-in-Publication Data

Heikkinen, Jaakko Santtu
Panpsychism and the Combination Problem

       p.   cm.
Includes bibliographical references.

ISBN 978-1734-8042-49 (pbk.: alk. paper)

1. Philosophy of mind

Printing number: 9 8 7 6 5 4 3 2 1

Printed in the United States of America on acid-free paper.

Preface 9

Chapter 1: An Introduction to Consciousness 11
    1.1 The Problem of Consciousness 11
    1.2 Panpsychism 14
    1.3 Phenomenal Consciousness 17

Chapter 2: Physicalism 21
    2.1 Defining Physicalism 21
    2.2 Fundamentality and Levels of Description 23
    2.3 Emergent Physicalism 26
    2.4 The Conceivability Argument 31
    2.5 The Argument from Intrinsic Natures 34
    2.6 Conclusion 42

Chapter 3: The Varieties of Panpsychism 43
    3.1 Defining Panpsychism 43
    3.2 Constitutive and Non-Constitutive Panpsychism 44
    3.3 Panpsychism and Panprotopsychism 49
    3.4 Smallism and Priority Cosmopsychism 51

Chapter 4: The Combination Problem 53
    4.1 The Subject-Summing Problem 55
    4.2 The Quality-Combination Problem 57
    4.3 The Structural Mismatch Problem 60

Chapter 5: Suggested Solutions to the Combination Problem 62
    5.1 The Non-Combinatorial Response 62
    5.1.1 Panpsychist Infusion 63
    5.2 Combinatorial Responses 72
    5.2.1 Phenomenal Bonding 73
    5.2.2 Priority Cosmopsychism 84
    5.2.3 The Theory of Natural Individuals 96

Chapter 6: Conclusions and Discussion 108

Bibliography 113

Index 121

Panpsychism
and the
Combination
Problem

PREFACE

This small book grew out of my master's thesis, written for the University of Helsinki in early 2019. The basic theme of the work is obvious from its title: the subject is panpsychism and the so-called *combination problem* that plagues it. In the course of this fairly technical presentation, the prevailing view of our times, physicalism, is also considered in great detail, especially in terms of its various problems. Many of these problems are such that they are quite easily remedied by the panpsychist position.

The present work is indeed quite technical, due to it having been originally tailored to an exclusively academic audience. I have expanded the introduction of the work greatly to accommodate the slightly more causal reader, and my hope is that even if you're not an actual expert in this specific field, you still might get something of interest out of the whole thing.

Nevertheless, I believe this book to work best as a fairly comprehensive, yet also concise introduction to panpsychism for those who are already relatively versed in the lingo and conventions of academic philosophy of mind. If you belong in this category, I hope the book serves your interests and leaves you with a deeper understanding of panpsychism and why it might act as an enticing alternative to more traditional physicalism; as well as of the major questions and problems still surrounding panpsychism.

I would like to take this opportunity to thank the supervisors of my master's thesis, Paavo Pylkkänen and Gabriel Sandu, for

PANPSYCHISM AND THE COMBINATION PROBLEM

their comments back when I was writing the original work. I would further like to thank Paavo for his valuable encouragement and validation throughout my studies. My thanks go also to Tuomas Tahko for some early feedback on the thesis. I wish to greatly thank David Skrbina for his invaluable aid in publishing this work as a separate book— the book was, essentially, David's idea, and without his help the whole thing would certainly not have come to pass.

I would also like to thank my family and my friends for their company during the time I was originally writing this work. My greatest thanks go to my life partner Anni, whose daily company provides me with so much joy, warmth, and meaning.

Finally, my thanks go to you, reader, for picking up this book and having a look inside. May your time with this work, be it short or lengthy, be fruitful, interesting, and enjoyable.

Santtu Heikkinen
30 November 2020
Helsinki, Finland

CHAPTER ONE

AN INTRODUCTION TO CONSCIOUSNESS

1.1 The Problem of Consciousness

During the last few hundred years humanity has achieved many incredible things in the fields of science and technology. Our knowledge of how nature works—the mechanisms underlying natural processes of all kinds—has increased to the point where our influence as a species reigns paramount over all nature. Naturally this influence is not only beneficial—technological innovations in the utilization of natural resources have also led to many unhealthy environmental consequences. But despite the dangers of modern technology, its potency remains clear: we are powerful, and we know much.

But there are certain areas of reality which still remain as mysterious as ever. One of these is *consciousness*, the existence of such a thing as experience. From the empirical viewpoint of the sciences, which observe reality from an external, third-person point of view, consciousness is nowhere to be seen. From the empirical viewpoint, reality appears to be mechanistic, a vast physical system with parts that interact based on set laws of nature. Even though this image, too, remains in part mysterious to the sciences—there is still much we don't understand about quantum mechanics, for example—it seems that there is no real need for consciousness to explain any part of it. Physical reality appears to be *causally closed*, meaning that all physical effects appear to have sufficient physical causes. Physical reality does not appear to need consciousness to work perfectly well.

So why talk about consciousness at all? The reason is simple: because we *are* conscious. We *do* have experiences. It is, to use a well-worn phrase by Thomas Nagel, *something it is like to be you*. And this something-it-is-like-to-be-ness, that is consciousness. You aren't just a robot, and neither am I. We are living, experiencing beings.

This is the mystery. Why are we conscious? What is consciousness? How can a physical system be conscious; what makes it conscious? The mystery here is deep enough that some[1] have taken it to be unsolvable in principle; perhaps we humans are, as limited beings, simply not capable of understanding the mystery. Then again there are others[2] who believe that the mystery may be solvable, but not by referring only to the realm of the physical as it is commonly understood. In other words, these thinkers believe that the mystery surrounding consciousness can be lifted, but only by approaching the problem from a different angle than physics and the other empirical sciences. The subject of this book—panpsychism—is an example of a view of this latter kind.

Perhaps the most common view of our time on consciousness is *emergent physicalism*, which claims that consciousness is an *emergent property* of physical systems: a property that appears in certain kinds of physical systems once an appropriate level of complexity or a specific kind of organization is reached. This view on consciousness and the genesis of experientiality sounds

---

[1] The so-called mysterianists, who argue that the mystery is essentially unsolvable. The leading contemporary proponent of this view in the field of philosophy is Colin McGinn (e.g. 2006).

[2] Influential examples are David Chalmers (1995) and Joseph Levine (1983), with a vast tradition following them.

CHAPTER ONE

reasonable enough at first glance, but more careful scrutiny has revealed significant problems.

For one, it would still remain a complete mystery *how* and *why* such a thing as conscious experience emerges from matter. At least in principle, a thorough physico-chemical explanation of the behavior of even us human beings requires no reference to consciousness. From the empirical perspective our nervous system appears as a configuration of nerve cells with their active and receptive connections, a plethora of neuro-transmitters activating electric impulses that spread out, connect and reconnect in the vastly complex machine that is our brain. This seems adequate in theory to explain the behavior of the organism, what makes it tick and do the things it does. Then why aren't we machines? What makes us conscious? Why isn't it, in reality, enough and adequate that we were simple automatons, without any inner life?

Secondly, if consciousness is an emergent phenomenon, when exactly does it emerge? In what conditions? Is the octopus—a highly intelligent creature exemplifying a decentralized nervous system very different to ours—conscious? What about a person with only half a brain, or one with just 10% of the brain matter as compared to an ordinary person, as with some severe hydrocephalus patients? Do split-brain cases, where the corpus callosum connecting the two hemispheres of the brain has been cut to treat e.g. severe epilepsy, constitute two separate conscious beings, since they seem to exhibit dual personalities with separate preferences and agendas?

This is a veritable tangle of questions that nevertheless only scrapes the surface of the problems facing emergent physicalism. These questions make up the *hard problem of consciousness* (so called following Chalmers 1995), also called the *explanatory gap* between the physical and the mental (following Levine 1983). Emergent physicalism also faces several other problems of a more analytical nature, which make up the primary subject of the first part of this book.

PANPSYCHISM AND THE COMBINATION PROBLEM

However, you want to look at things, and whatever your current beliefs on this matter may be, it is clear that there is here a mystery, there is here a question worthy of an answer. In our seeking for that answer, we ought to look at the alternatives, explore views which, though they may clash with the presuppositions and established beliefs of our particular culture, may nonetheless reveal to us better ways of approaching this question. Panpsychism is one such view.

1.2 Panpsychism

Panpsychism is—to simplify things radically—the view that *everything is conscious*[3]. Experientiality is everywhere, a fundamental facet of reality. Panpsychism thus solves many of the problems of emergence: there is no mystery about the function of consciousness, nor about its genesis, since consciousness has always already been there. It's part of what it means to exist.

Panpsychism as a research program aims to deliver elucidation on at least the following two major philosophical conundrums. The first of these is the ontological substance question: what is the substance of reality, that is, *what exactly exists*, what are things ultimately made of. Panpsychism acts as an alternative to materialism (the idea that matter is all there is) and substance dualism (which takes mind and matter to be entirely separate substances[4]). The second major question on which panpsychism gives an answer is the *mind-body problem*. This is the question of how exactly mental entities, events and properties are related to physical entities, events and properties—in other words, what is the relationship between the mind and the body. These two questions are interconnected, and explanatory power in

---

[3] A more exact definition will be given later in the book, in chapter 3.1.

[4] Substance dualism has several extremely difficult problems of its own, which I shall (somewhat briefly) touch upon in chapter 3.2.

CHAPTER ONE

answering the second question is a prime reason to favor a particular answer to the first question.

The program of panpsychism aims to give elegant answers to the problems of consciousness, and to find a proper, relevant and coherent place for consciousness in nature. A few common misconceptions should be discarded right off the bat: the idea here is *not* that e.g. rocks, mountains or the Eiffel tower are conscious beings, for the conscious matter constituting them might not combine into the kinds of coherent unities that human beings exemplify[5]. In other words, not all things we can name and point to in the world are necessarily conscious *subjects* of experience. We have named these objects as distinct parts of reality primarily because of their functional usefulness to us, and there is no reason why usefulness to humans would correlate with experiential unity or subjectivity. However, at the very least the most elementary, the most fundamental parts of reality, are conscious subjects. Whether these turn out to be the elementary particles we currently see descriptions of in physics is an open question; things might turn out very differently in the end. But whatever the fundamental "ground level" of reality turns out to be, that level *at least* has to include conscious subjects. In this way, at the very least, consciousness is everywhere.

Let's clarify another common misconception: the idea is *not* that everything has conscious experience that is *alike* to human experience; the panpsychist is not ascribing e.g. thought or emotion to an elementary particle (or whatever the fundamental beings may be). But *something*—it is *something* it is like to be an elementary particle, there is *something* there akin to experience in a very primitive form. Otherwise, consciousness remains an

---

[5] This is not to say that panpsychism in any way implies that they couldn't be conscious subjects either. Some philosophers have historically held the view that rocks and other natural formations do make up conscious subjects. A somewhat recent example is J. Baird Callicott (1982). Skrbina (2017) seems to also be quite sympathetic to the view.

eternal mystery. At a fundamental level matter itself has to be conscious in a way that allows it to combine in various ways to compose larger unities.

Though the idea of panpsychism may seem alien to our contemporary sensibilities, historically panpsychism has not been without its exponents. In fact, panpsychism has arguably been the majority view on consciousness for the better part of history! Plato, Spinoza, Leibniz, Schopenhauer, Nietzsche, Peirce—these are just some examples of major philosophers who have explicitly argued for the panpsychist view[6]. Panpsychism fell out of favor during the anti-metaphysical logical positivism of the 20th century but has again gained significant traction within the last ten years and can now be taken to be the single most serious contender to emergent physicalism in metaphysics and the philosophy of mind.

The structure of the book is as follows. The following introductory parts will explain some relevant basic concepts of consciousness, further reinforcing the foundation for the rest of the book. The second, significantly longer part is an analytical exploration of the relative theoretical demerits of physicalism, establishing the motivation for panpsychism. The third part gives a definition of panpsychism and explores the varieties of panpsychism in terms of three conceptual axes: constitutivism/ non-constitutivism, panpsychism/panprotopsychism, and smallism/ priority cosmopsychism. The fourth chapter goes on to describe the most serious objection to panpsychism in contemporary debate, the combination problem, as well as its sub-problems as they are often presented in current discussion. The fifth chapter then explores several of the most advocated and discussed suggestions for a panpsychist framework in depth, touching on their most relevant merits and demerits as well as how they manage to answer the

---

[6] The most comprehensive account of the history of panpsychism in Western philosophy is David Skrbina's excellent Panpsychism in the West (2017).

combination problem and its sub-problems. The sixth and final part is formed of an end discussion, including the major conclusions of the book, as well as suggestions for further work.

Before we go on to consider physicalism in more detail, some explanatory remarks on the concept of consciousness are in order. There are several different ways to use the term consciousness, of which the most relevant here is *phenomenal consciousness*.

1.3 Phenomenal Consciousness

Phenomenality means essentially the same thing as experientiality: the existence of experiences, that is, conscious *phenomena*. Phenomenal consciousness pertains to the actual existence of conscious experience, the seemingly indubitable fact that there is experience of some kind, taken in the broadest sense possible. A famous and much-used way of elucidating the concept of phenomenal consciousness is to say that a thing is phenomenally conscious if and only if *it is like something to be that thing*[7]. For example, it is plausible that though the senses and perceptual mechanisms of a bat are very different from those of a human, the bat is not merely a machine with no inner or mental life; the bat, as a living creature, plausibly has experiences of some kind. It is literally something it is like to be a bat. Phenomenal consciousness pertains to a global state of experientiality, of there being such phenomena as experiences. It can also be described as the state of there being a subjective, first person point of view, or of qualities being *presented* to a subject as experiences.

Following a distinction made by Ned Block (1995), the phenomenal concept of consciousness is often contrasted with *access consciousness*, which pertains to the availability of

---

[7] This manner of description was made famous by Thomas Nagel in his 1974 classic article "What is it like to be a bat?", although Goff (2017a) traces its original appearance to Sprigge & Montefiore (1971).

particular information to be used in reasoning and for guiding behavior and action. Michael Cerullo (2015) makes a similar distinction between non-cognitive and cognitive consciousness, where non-cognitive pertains, again, to a global state of experientiality (i.e. phenomenal consciousness), and cognitive pertains to specific cognitive and rational functioning (i.e. access consciousness). Although the question about the necessary and sufficient conditions for access consciousness is an interesting topic of inquiry as well, the debate concerning panpsychism is by far primarily concerned with the criteria for phenomenal consciousness, and whether or not such criteria can be given.

Following C. S. Peirce (1866/1982), phenomenal consciousness has traditionally been taken to consist of its own kind of properties or aspects, called *qualia*. The blueness of the sky, the smell of fresh coffee and the touch of a woolen cloth on your skin are examples of qualia. A similar concept that has especially been used in the literature of the first half of the 20th century is that of sense-data, referring to the mental objects and representations that we are directly aware of, in contrast to the ungraspable *noumenon* of the objective world behind them (e.g. Russell 1912). Even though the existence of qualia is somewhat controversial in contemporary literature (e.g. Dennett 1990 makes the argument that a naturalistic conception of the mind has no room and no need for the concept of quale), phenomenal consciousness is not quite so controversial[8]— Strawson (2006a, 2016), for example, takes the existence of

---

[8] Though so-called eliminative materialists are sometimes taken to advocate complete eliminativism about phenomenal consciousness, what they are aiming for is more of an eliminativism about folk-psychological concepts dealing with phenomenality (Ramsey 2013). Eliminativists thus argue for the completeness of natural scientific, or more narrowly (and popularly), physical description—and furthermore, that consciousness can ultimately be completely and satisfyingly explained using the methodologies of third-person empirical science (e.g. Churchland 2013 p. 57–58).

CHAPTER ONE

phenomenal consciousness to be so obvious as to be irrefutable, while Goff (2017a) presents the following principle as a necessary axiom of any realistic philosophical system (p. 3):

> *The Consciousness Constraint*—Any adequate theory of reality must entail that at least some phenomenal concepts are satisfied. (A concept is satisfied when it truly corresponds to reality, for example, the concept of God is satisfied if and only if God exists.)

I shall follow this trend by adopting Goff's Consciousness Constraint (TCC) in this work. The existence of phenomenality seems to me to be our most fundamental epistemic starting point. Pierre Gassendi writes in his contemporary commentary on Descartes' famous *cogito, ergo sum* argument that, though the existence of an actual thinking *subject* be dubitable, the "claim that is indubitable is the agent-independent claim that there is cognitive activity present" (Fisher 2014). When we think or perceive anything, there is *something* going on that is presented to us or appears to us, our experience of that event. I agree with Strawson (2016) that any real naturalist must be a realist about experience, because experience is the first thing any scientist encounters when they try to do science (p. 84). However, it has to be stated clearly that this is, ultimately, a matter completely outside of co-operative empirical investigation: the existence of experience is a fundamentally private datum, unavailable for public presentation. It remains on the shoulders of each to verify for themselves that there is *something* going on in their inner life, some way that their life is presented to them as experiences; that there are, indeed, such phenomena as phenomena. Any reader that disagrees with this result is free to question the entire enterprise of panpsychism and consciousness research in general. However, I feel that I have personally verified this matter in my own life to

PANPSYCHISM AND THE COMBINATION PROBLEM

a degree satisfactory to motivate analytical work founded on this assumption, and I am certainly not alone in attempting to build upon this bedrock. Thus, the Consciousness Constraint shall accordingly be our "fundamental axiom, the Archimedean fixed point around which all else revolves", to paraphrase Goff's turn of phrase (2017a, p. 4).

The existence of phenomenal consciousness shall then be our starting point. The crucial focus of this work will be on an exploration of panpsychism and the combination problem. But to motivate such an exploration, we first have to inspect its greatest contemporary rival, the jumping-off point from which contemporary panpsychism has evolved. This rival is physicalism. In the meanwhile, we will also gather up and inspect various tools necessary for further exploring the theoretical merits and deficits of panpsychism.

CHAPTER TWO

PHYSICALISM

2.1 Defining Physicalism

Panpsychism acts as an alternative to the age-old trio of materialism, idealism and dualism as an explanatory framework to answer the mind-body problem. In the course of this book out of these three rivals *materialism,* especially in the form of *physicalism*, is foremost, since it is by far the most popular view both in contemporary philosophy (as studied by Bourget & Chalmers 2014, p. 15) as well as in contemporary neuroscience.

Physicalism—roughly the idea that everything is fundamentally physical—is arguably an essential component of the philosophical 'received view' of modern times. However, as Goff (2017a, p. 23) points out, it is ironic that a more sophisticated definition of the doctrine seems elusive. This question of definition ultimately dictates what the relationship between physicalism and other views are—for example, the relationship between physicalism and panpsychism. Even though panpsychism is often contrasted with materialism as a doctrine (e.g. Brüntrup 2016, Chalmers 2016, Goff 2017a), some panpsychists characterize it as a particular form of materialism. Galen Strawson (2006a, 2016), for example, argues that any "realistic" materialist framework—by which he means any theory that accepts phenomenal consciousness as an ineliminable facet of reality—necessarily entails panpsychism; and thereby considers panpsychistic monism[9] a form of materialism. Strawson (2016) further considers himself explicitly a physicalist on the grounds that he agrees that the laws and dictates of fundamental physics[10] apply to all things in existence, even though physics is not alone adequate for a complete description of reality. (p. 85–86). In contrast to this, Philip Goff (2017a) considers his view (and all panpsychism) anti-physicalist because he disagrees that the language, terminology and theory of physics can completely describe reality without any reference to mental or phenomenal kinds (p. 40). Strawson thereby defines physicalism as the thesis that the laws and theory of physics apply to all things, whereas Goff defines it as the conjunction of two theses: that the terminology and methodology of physics are adequate for a complete description of reality and its fundamental facts[11]; and that the fundamental facts of reality do not include or involve facts about the phenomenal (or, to be exact, even the *protophenomenal*, meaning a kind of proto-mentality that is not quite consciousness, but "close enough"; I discuss protophenomenality later on in chapter 3.2). Since the contrast between anti-panpsychist monism and panpsychist monism is philosophically fruitful and essential to the motivation and defense of panpsychism, I shall define *physicalism* in the more restricted way:

---

[9] Though panpsychism can usually be characterized as monist in spirit, a substance dualist panpsychist position is still conceptualy coherent. However, there currently do not seem to me to be many proponents of a substance dualist panpsychism, although early Chalmers (1995) had some sympathy for the view.

[10] I follow Ladyman & Ross (2007) in defining fundamental physics to mean "that part of physics about which measurements taken anywhere in the universe carry information" (p. 55), viz. the part of physics that deals with the widest possible scope of phenomena.

[11] Strawson (2006a) in fact delineates between these two conceptions of physicalism, calling the former, wider version "physicalism", and the latter, narrower version endorsed by Goff "physicSalism" (p. 4).

CHAPTER TWO

Physicalism: The doctrine or view that the terminology and methodology of physics can provide a complete description of reality and its fundamental facts without any reference to the phenomenal or the protophenomenal.

This shall be our working definition of physicalism, a counterpoise to panpsychism. In contrast, I accept *materialism* as a broader doctrine compatible with panpsychism, as merely any variant of substance monism which includes the negation of anti-realism about mind-independent reality[12], thus excluding only substance dualism as well as those variants of subjective idealism that consider everyday reality as mere appearance.

2.2 Fundamentality and Levels of Description

The word *fundamental* has thus far appeared several times in the text, as it does in our above definition of physicalism. It is helpful to examine this term in more depth.

Some fact or entity X is fundamental if its obtainment (in the case of a fact) or existence (in the case of an entity) is not *grounded* in any other fact or entity. Grounding in metaphysics pertains to a non-causal relation of asymmetric determination, an *in-virtue-of* relation in the sense of some X obtaining *in virtue of* some Y obtaining, where X and Y can either one be a fact or property or a group of facts or properties, and where this relation is not causal (e.g. Bliss & Trogdon 2016). Grounding is, in other words, a relation of ontological dependence, and hierarchical by its very nature: a less fundamental sort of fact or thing is always

---

[12] I am here referring to the complex kinds of minds that humans and potentially other higher organisms have. Mentality or phenomenality in the widest possible sense is postulated to be ubiquitous in panpsychist frameworks, so in this wider sense the panpsychist would also consider reality to be thoroughly mind-dependent.

grounded in a more fundamental sort of fact or thing (ibid.). Thus, for example, we would say that the fact that there is a party is grounded in the fact that there are people reveling, drinking, eating, mingling and so on (Goff 2017a, p. 45), and the fact that a particle is accelerating is grounded in the fact that its velocity is increasing over time (Fine 2012, p. 39).

These are both examples of *grounding by analysis,* which is the standard form of grounding employed in the literature[13]; the less fundamental fact (the fact that there is a party; the fact that a particle is accelerating) is grounded in the more fundamental fact (reveling, etc.; increasing velocity) in virtue of the former being analyzable losslessly into the latter. The less fundamental fact is logically entailed by the more fundamental, being already implicitly present in the latter, and in this sense ultimately contributes nothing *over-and-above* the more fundamental fact or facts. Any theory describing all the fundamental facts of nature is then immediately also able to describe all the facts of nature in general, due to all non-fundamental facts being losslessly analyzable to the fundamental facts. The ultimately fundamental facts or entities are thereby the facts and entities that have no further ground; the facts and entities in which all else is implicit, the defining ground of being.

Physicalism as defined above is then the doctrine that the terminology and methodology of physics are adequate for a complete, lossless description of the facts and entities that ground all other facts and entities, the 'fundamental level' of reality, without any reference to the phenomenal (or the protophenomenal); which has, as its immediate consequence, that all facts in general are analyzable to physical facts. In practice, this usually takes the

---

[13] We shall introduce another notion of grounding, grounding by subsumption, in chapter 5.3. Grounding by subsumption is essentially the priority monist counterpart to grounding by analysis. For the current discussion the concept of grounding by analysis will suffice.

CHAPTER TWO

form of a belief that all there 'really' is is a fundamental layer of *microphysical* elementary particles, events or properties—in other words, that *microphysical facts* are the fundamental ground for all other facts[14]. *Macrophysical facts* are then those facts which have to do with non-fundamental physical objects, including everyday objects such as tables, rocks and physical human bodies, which are respectively called macrophysical objects.

The phenomenal counterparts to these concepts of micro- and macrophysical facts are *microphenomenal* facts and *macrophenomenal* facts. The microphenomenal pertains to the potential phenomenal aspects, properties or natures of the microphysical. This could, for example, include whatever phenomenal properties or aspects the ultimate elementary particles of physics would involve. The macrophenomenal then pertains to the facts which have to do with composite phenomenal entities and events, including the properties of human (and animal) phenomenal consciousness.

The physicalist considers *all macrophenomenal facts* having to deal with human (and animal) consciousness to also *be grounded in the fundamental microphysical facts* without postulating the microphenomenal at all. Considered from the most common physicalist viewpoint, *emergent physicalism*, consciousness is an *emergent* property of purely physical reality, arising from the purely physical once a sufficient level of complexity is reached.

---

[14] This conception, as well as the corresponding alternative of constitutive panpsychism discussed below in the main text as well as further in 3.2, relies on a common but not necessary premise, smallism: the idea that the smallest constituents of reality, the mereological atoms or simples, are the grounding base of reality (Coleman 2006, 2016)). Montero (2006, p. 181) calls the same doctrine fundamentalism, the view that the smallest, non-decomposable components of reality are the most fundamental. The distinction between smallist/fundamentalist panpsychism and its alternatives is considered in depth in chapter 3.4.

2.3 Emergent Physicalism

The idea of emergent physicalism is that phenomenal experience somehow emerges out of unconscious and phenomenally inanimate matter. This is to say that, although phenomenal properties are purely physical phenomena and losslessly grounded in the microphysical, they are ontologically novel in the sense that they do not appear at all in lower levels of physical complexity. But when the required complexity is reached, nothing over-and-above the physical grounding base is needed for the appearance of phenomenality. This idea, though very common in both contemporary neuroscience and the popular imagination[15], has some remarkable problems. We shall first elucidate the matter with some conceptual distinctions concerning emergence.

Chalmers (2006) offers an illuminating distinction between weak and strong emergence. By *weak emergence* he means the appearance of seemingly novel phenomena in conditions where this appearance is, in principle, understandable *a priori*. Weak emergence implies grounding—a weakly emergent thing is always ontologically grounded in something more fundamental. Thus, in weak emergence the emergent thing is always a logically entailed result of something more fundamental. *Strong emergence*, on the other hand, is the appearance of novel phenomena in conditions where this appearance is even in principle not understandable *a priori*[16]. In view of the explanatory gap between what are traditionally held as the physical and the phenomenal, it seems that the emergence of the phenomenal from the non-phenomenal would be, at the very least, an instance of strong emergence.

---

[15] Enqvist (1998), for example, delivers a description of consciousness much like this, aimed at a popular audience.

[16] Frank Jackson (2006) makes a similar distinction between a priori emergence and a posteriori emergence, being fairly close to synonymous with weak and strong emergence, respectively.

CHAPTER TWO

The question of whether such strong, *a posteriori* emergence is generally plausible or not remains up to debate. However, Brüntrup (2016) adds another distinction to the concepts of emergence, distinguishing strong emergence from what he calls *superstrong emergence*. For Brüntrup, strong emergence means pretty much the same as it does for Chalmers: *a posteriori* emergence that is unexpected and without the inclusion of an asymmetric grounding relation. But there is a further qualification, that strong emergence is still always *intra-attribute* emergence. By this Brüntrup means that the emergence base and the emergent property are both within the broadly same categorical domain. The emergence of something physical from the physical, even if it were *a posteriori,* would be at most an instance of strong emergence, since both the base and the emergent property are within the same categorical domain of physicality.

In contrast, something is superstrongly emergent if the emergence is *inter-attribute* emergence, emergence of a property of one categorical domain from a base of a different categorical domain. Such emergence would require its own kind of *ad hoc* nomology, brute and unexplainable laws connecting the emergent property and the emergence base[17]. The emergence of something from nothing would be a prime example of superstrong emergence, as would the emergence of something concrete in a world otherwise purely made of abstract entities. The *radical emergence* of Galen Strawson (2006a) is essentially a synonymous concept, referring to inter-attribute emergence that is even in principle inscrutable, and giving the emergence of something spatially extended from something non-extended as an example. Both writers use their respective concepts to delineate a

---

[17] C.D. Broad's (1925) trans-ordinal laws are conceptually quite close to the kind of laws strong emergence would require. His concept of intra-ordinal laws would respectively hold roughly for the kind of nomology involved in weak emergence.

type of emergence so unexplainable that it ought to be considered untenable. With these tools in hand our next task is to evaluate the plausibility of emergent physicalism.

First of all, our inherited conception of what it means to be material seems to be at odds with what we take to be phenomenal, our own domain of conscious experience. Strawson (2006a) writes that, even though in the material domain there are many instances of emergence that are arguably quite coherent and understandable to us, such as the emergence of the liquidity of water from its constituent molecules of H_2O[18], the emergence of the phenomenal domain from a phenomenally inanimate material domain is not even in principle understandable to us. The relevant difference is, according to Strawson, the following: In the case of water, the emergence of liquidity is wholly dependent on the properties of the molecules that make up the water, and their interaction. We might plausibly be able to reduce the liquidity of water to the properties and interaction of its constituent molecules and explain liquidity with reference to these properties and interaction. In other words, water is liquid in virtue of the microphysical properties of its constituent elements; its liquidity is grounded in the microphysical properties of its constituent elements, which seem to necessitate the emergence of the macrophysical property of liquidity. This would, in Chalmers' distinction, count as weak emergence, since the emergent property is grounded in its emergence base. However, in the case of phenomenality, there is nothing in the non-phenomenal material base that phenomenality would seem to be similarly dependent on. According to Strawson, we cannot even in principle reduce the phenomenal to the non-phenomenal in an understandable way. (2006a, pp. 9–10).

---

[18] It has to be said that emergence of chemical macro-properties such as liquidity is not certainly as easy to understand as Strawson's portrayal of things might imply, though the point still stands that they may remain understandable in principle.

CHAPTER TWO

Furthermore, the natural sciences do not seem to have any room for experientiality, a situation which is often described in terms of the principle of the causal closure of the physical domain, according to which, if a physical event is caused, it always has sufficient physical causes and a wholly physical causal explanation (e.g. Kim 2011, p. 112). The causal closure of the physical is one of the principal problems facing substance dualism ever since the times of Descartes: if every physical event has sufficient physical causes, what work is there left for the mental to do? Dualism is thereby immediately threatened by *epiphenomenalism*, that is, the causal inefficacy of the mental; and though interactionism remains a conceptually possible doctrine, it faces significant problems having to do with causal overdetermination and strong commitments to a particular future physics (Chalmers 2016a p. 24), as well as the classical argument from the discontinuity of the spatial and the nonspatial (Robinson 2017). Emergent physicalism faces essentially the same problem: if physical facts and events are sufficient to explain all empirically observable events, and phenomenal facts and events are all losslessly grounded by analysis in the physical, there seems to be little role for the phenomenal to play[19]—and the plausibility of causally irrelevant yet entirely physically described properties is questionable at best[20].

In addition, since nothing in the physical domain seems to necessitate the existence of the phenomenal in any way, it is

---

[19] It might be possible to somehow argue that the "higher-level" phenomenal properties somehow 'inherit' the causal relevance of their physical grounding base. Brüntrup (2016, pp. 60–64) argues at some length against such a view on the basis of the strong logical asymmetry between the grounding base and the higher-level properties.

[20] As we shall see in chapter 2.5, causally irrelevant yet physically described properties are actually not only questionable, but veritably oxymoronic, since the descriptions of physics are always limited purely to the causal and the dispositional.

difficult to coherently and understandably explain the emergence of the phenomenal, for there seems to be nothing in our current material science in virtue of which phenomenal consciousness would be generated. We cannot find the ground of the phenomenal in the non-phenomenal in any intuitive and obvious way. It has thus proven to be difficult for emergentists to give working sufficient and necessary conditions for consciousness to appear in a physical system; where to draw the line, and why? Is an octopus with a relatively decentralized nervous system conscious? Are split-brain patients, whose behavior seems to imply two separate cognitive agents with separate motivations and separate foci of attention (e.g. Gazzaniga 2005, p. 654), formed of two distinct and separate consciousnesses? Is half a brain enough for phenomenal consciousness?

David Skrbina (2011) has framed these questions facing the emergentist with a division into three kinds of questions: the historical, the phylogenic, and the ontogenic. The historical questions concern *when* and *why* consciousness appeared in the course of evolution, if it hasn't been there all along. Presumably its sudden appearance in reality would have to be the result of some clear evolutionary advantage to its bearers, and there should be a fairly definite point in history at which consciousness initially emerged into being. The phylogenic questions concern *which organisms* partake of consciousness—which beings are conscious, and which are not, and why the line is to be drawn there. The ontogenic questions concern the conditions in which consciousness emerges into a particular organism, such as how many neurons does a fetus need before it becomes conscious. The problem is that the emergentist can't seem to answer any of these questions properly—yet they all ought to be answered for the emergentist thesis to become plausible (p. 118–119).

Because of all these problems described above, the only way to currently see the emergence of the phenomenal from the non-phenomenal is as an instance of radical emergence: emergence that cannot even in principle be understood, explained or predicted in any way. But radical emergence is indeed very suspect. Radical or superstrong emergence leaves nature discontinuous, and such qualitative discontinuity ought to be rejected. *Natura non facit saltus,* as the Leibnizian axiom goes—nature makes no leaps.

2.4 The Conceivability Argument

An additional problem facing the emergent physicalist, as well as any physicalist respecting the Consciousness Constraint and thereby endorsing the existence of the phenomenal, is the *conceivability argument*, most famously known as the *zombie argument*, following Chalmers' (1996) initial systematic treatment of the idea. The conceivability argument, in its most simple form (roughly following Chalmers 2016a, p. 23), is as follows:

The Conceivability Argument

(1) It is conceivable that the sum of all physical facts P can hold without any phenomenal fact Q holding (it is conceivable that P & not-Q).
(2) If P & not-Q is conceivable, it is metaphysically possible.
(3) If P & not-Q is metaphysically possible, physicalism is false.
(4) Therefore, physicalism is false[21].

---

[21] In the famous zombie formulation, P would be all the physical facts having to do with a human being whereas Q would be the fact that that human being is phenomenally conscious. P & not-Q would thereby make her a philosophical zombie.

The first premise involves *negative ideal conceivability* instead of the positive, imaginative conceivability of common parlance, where something is considered conceivable if it can be imagined. A sentence S is negatively ideally conceivable if and only if it is not *a priori* that S is false. Negative ideal conceivability is thus defined through a negation—it *cannot* be *a priori* that S is false, for S to be conceivable in this way—hence it is negative; and it does not depend on the powers of human imagination, hence it is ideal. No amount of *a priori* reasoning could rule it out. (Goff 2017a, pp. 81–82). The first premise is thus logically identical with the sentence: "it is not a priori that not-(P & not-Q)". Taken in this sense the premise seems intuitive, since it rests on the apparent epistemic gap between the physical and the phenomenal: if no amount of *a priori* reasoning can lead us from the physical facts to any phenomenal fact Q[22], no amount of *a priori* reasoning from the physical could rule Q out either.

The third premise is also very straightforward: if physicalism entails, as in the definition given above in chapter 2.1, that all fundamental facts are physical facts (i.e. describable in the language of physics), all phenomenal facts should be groundable by analysis to physical facts. However, as was explained in chapter 2.2, grounding by analysis implies logical entailment *a priori* from the more fundamental to the less fundamental—and therefore it should not be possible that P and not-Q. If it is possible physicalism is false.

The second premise is the trickiest. The jump from negative ideal conceivability to metaphysical possibility is a contested claim, called the *conceivability principle* (e.g. Goff 2017a, p. 77). In its simplest form, the conceivability principle suggests that if a

---

[22] This is basically the now-classical knowledge argument involving Mary, the brilliant neuroscientist who learns all the physical facts concerning color but yet knows not what seeing red is actually like, introduced by Frank Jackson (1982).

sentence is conceivably true, then it is possibly true. This most simple version of the principle comes under attack from the counterexample of *a posteriori necessities*, in the vein of Kripke (e.g. 1980) and Putnam (e.g. 1975). According to Kripke and Putnam, the essence of water is H_2O, and moreover that this is a metaphysical necessity; the essence of water could not be XYZ. The fact that "water is H_2O" is *a posteriori*. Since the negation of all *a posteriori* facts is conceivable, the idea that "water is XYZ" is conceivable. Therefore there are facts, such as "water is XYZ", which are metaphysically impossible, yet they are conceivable.

Chalmers (2009) attempts to address this flaw by a *two-dimensional* semantics, which posits that terms such as "water" have two distinct intensions, a primary one and a secondary one. The primary intension captures the *appearance property* of the referent, which in the case of water could be approximated by something like "the liquid, translucent stuff that rains from the sky, gathers in seas and lakes and is vital for plant and animal life". The secondary intension captures the actual essence of the term, which in the case of water could be approximated as "being made of H_2O molecules"[23]. Chalmers' idea is to modify the conceivability principle into a two-dimensional version: If a sentence is conceivably true, then its *primary intension* is true in some possible world. The essence of water can thereby be necessary *a posteriori*, leaving it still conceivable *a priori* that something else that fulfils its primary intension—the appearance property of something being, for lack of a better word, *watery*—could possibly have a different essence also, such as being composed of XYZ molecules.

Chalmers then refers to Kripke (1980) in defense of the Direct Reference Thesis: that although in our usual parlance

---

[23] It has to be emphasized that this is indeed a gross and amateurish simplification, and should not be taken to represent the actual essence of water.

physical and empirical concepts like "water" pick out their referents in terms of their appearance properties (such as whatever properties constitute "wateriness"), phenomenal concepts do not pick out their referents in terms of their appearance properties, but in terms of their essential properties (they *refer directly* to the essence, hence, the Direct Reference Thesis). The idea is that with phenomenal concepts there are no separate primary and secondary intensions: the essence of a phenomenal concept or notion *is* its appearance. Let us next see how the conjunction of two-dimensional semantics and the Direct Reference Thesis help us in avoiding the counterargument from *a posteriori* necessities.

The first premise of the conceivability argument was that it is negatively ideally conceivable that the sum of all physical facts P could hold without any phenomenal fact Q holding—that physical facts do not *a priori* entail phenomenal facts. The revised second premise, using Chalmers' two-dimensional semantics, is that if something is negatively ideally conceivable, its primary intension is metaphysically possible. If the Direct Reference Thesis then holds, the primary and secondary intensions of phenomenal concepts are identical. Since the sentence P & not-Q does not include only phenomenal terms, but also physical terms, for the sentence P & not-Q to have identical primary and secondary intensions, the facts of theoretical physics must also have identical primary and secondary intensions. As Goff (2017a) writes, since the facts of theoretical physics are mathematico-nomic in nature—that is, they involve only mathematical and causal or dispositional concepts—this is arguably the case; mathematical and nomic concepts do not have an appearance property separate from their essence. (p. 90). Therefore, since both the phenomenal as well as the physical terms in P & not-Q have identical primary and secondary intensions, and the primary intension of the sentence is thus metaphysically possible, the

CHAPTER TWO

secondary intension of the sentence P & not-Q is also metaphysically possible, that is, it is true in some possible world; and hence, physicalism is false.

The physicalist has at least one more avenue for counterargument, however, and this is to say that phenomenal concepts do not refer to anything substantive in their referents. The idea is that phenomenal concepts have no primary or secondary intension; that they are what Goff (2017a) describes as "radically opaque" concepts (p. 91). Brian McLaughlin (2001) expresses essentially the same idea by categorizing phenomenal concepts into nondescriptive name concepts and type-demonstrative concepts, where concepts of neither category reveal anything essential about their referents, but simply name or demonstrate them (p. 324). Though this is again a debate deep enough for a lengthy discussion, suffice it here to say that although there might be some merit to this line of argumentation, it seems to many (as well as myself) highly intuitive to think that phenomenal concepts, such as pain, do refer to something substantive. This is called the principle of *revelation,* following Strawson (2006b); that our experience of phenomenal properties is such that their essence is directly revealed to us in that experience[24]. Our concepts refer to these essences, and are thereby not to be considered radically opaque.

Unlike the physicalist, the panpsychist does not fall prey to the conceivability argument. She avoids the problem by admitting that though all the facts of theoretical physics do not entail any phenomenal fact, this is because they are limited in their scope to a description of the purely *structural* properties of reality. Though structural zombies—entities sharing all the structural properties of their non-zombie, conscious counterparts, but not their

---

[24] Goff (2017a, pp. 106—132) presents a comprehensive analytical defence of revelation, the delving into which would take too much space in the present work.

phenomenal properties—may be possible, *categorical* zombies sharing all the properties of their non-zombie counterparts are not. This rests on a more sophisticated notion of what it is for something to be physical.

A relevant distinction here is one between the *narrowly physical* and the *broadly physical*. Chalmers (2016a) defines *narrowly physical* properties as the *dispositional* and *structural* properties completely describable in the mathematico-nomic concepts of physical theory. *Broadly physical* properties are whatever properties realize the narrowly physical dispositional and structural properties—in other words, whatever properties act as the categorical bases for those dispositional and structural properties, whatever carries them or instantiates them. (pp. 27–28, 33–36). Narrowly physical and broadly physical facts are correspondingly facts about narrowly physical properties and broadly physical properties.

Another, similar distinction, originally proposed by Daniel Stoljar (2001), is that between *t-physical* and *o-physical* properties. T-physical properties (where T stands for "theory") are those explicitly invoked by and considered in physical theory, such as mass, spin, or charge. These are, from the point of view of physics, exactly dispositional and relational properties—they refer to the dispositions of theoretical objects such as electrons and photons to act in particular ways and to be observed in particular ways; that is, they refer to the causal powers of entities that are theoretically postulated as their carriers. T-physical properties are essentially *extrinsic*. In contrast, o-physical properties (where O stands for "object") form the *intrinsic* nature of objects, what things actually *are* instead of just what they *do*. These are the categorical properties which act as the carriers of the T-physical causal powers and dispositions; the intrinsic properties, of which physics is by necessity completely silent. (p. 253–258).

CHAPTER TWO

The panpsychist line of argument is that though the conjunction of all *narrowly* physical facts may not entail a single phenomenal fact, the conjunction of all *broadly* physical facts—all extrinsic, dispositional, structural facts *plus* all the categorical, intrinsic facts—does entail the conjunction of all phenomenal facts. Only zombies sharing all narrowly physical properties with their conscious counterparts are conceivable; zombies sharing all broadly physical properties with their conscious counterparts are not. This is equivalent to saying that the extrinsic, t-physical properties of philosophical zombies are conceivably identical to those of non-zombies, but the intrinsic, o-physical properties are not. The panpsychist postulates that the intrinsic properties of concrete matter are exactly its phenomenal properties, of which empirical, third-person science cannot but remain silent. This silence of the natural sciences concerning the intrinsic nature of concrete, physical reality is the basis of the *argument from intrinsic natures* for panpsychism.

2.5 The Argument from Intrinsic Natures

Panpsychism with its variants is also referred to as *Russellian monism* after Bertrand Russell, who, in his 1927 monograph *Analysis of Matter*, explored the idea that all the natural sciences, for all their explanatory and practical power, only reveal to us the causal and nomic structure of reality and its constituent matter (Russell 1927, p. 254)—whereas the intrinsic, "deep" or categorical nature of matter remains hidden and unknown[25]. The natural

---

[25] It has to be said, however, that Russell's own final version of his "neutral monism" is unclear; according to e.g. Alter and Nagasawa (2012) his views varied greatly over decades, although the basic principle about the limitations of the natural sciences remained constant. Brüntrup (2016) warns against identifying panpsychism with Russellian monism due to Russell's explicit advocacy of agnosticism as comes to the intrinsic nature of reality (Russell 1927, p. 270).

sciences are framed in a language of mathematical concepts on one hand, and nomic concepts—meaning concepts of causation, natural necessity, or natural law—on the other (e.g. Goff 2017a, pp. 29–31). As described briefly in the last chapter, physics and the other natural, empirical sciences are concerned only with the narrowly physical dispositional and structural properties of matter—what things *do*, instead of what things *are*[26]. This means that the way that a material entity exists in itself, by itself—its *quiddity*, to use a traditional term in metaphysics, its *"what it is to be"*—does not concern the mathematico-nomic approach of physics and the other natural sciences. This is an immediate result of their dependence on externally verifiable, third-person data—all the data we can gather about any entity from the third-person perspective is the result of the effects that entity has on us and our measuring equipment, that is to say, a result off its causal powers and dispositional properties. Hence, the natural sciences can only reveal to us facts about the causal/nomic and relational structure of the world, leaving us completely in the dark as comes to its intrinsic nature. This has led some writers to abandon the idea of intrinsic natures altogether. Ladyman et al. (2007), for example, defend a metaphysics of mere relational structure—a framework rejecting individual relata on top of the relations between them—exactly on the grounds that theoretical physics makes no reference to individuals or their intrinsic properties[27].

The intuition that there must be relata to carry their relations

---

[26] William Seager (2006) expresses the same point: "If someone asks what an electron is, all we can say is that it is a 'particle' with a certain mass, electric charge, spin etc. Each of these attributes can only be defined relationally and all we know about them is what these relations provide." (p. 134).

[27] "Given that there is no a priori way of demonstrating that the world must be composed of individuals with intrinsic natures, and given that our best physics [makes no reference to them]… we reject them altogether." p. 154.

CHAPTER TWO

is strong, however, and has been extensively argued for especially as comes to the manifestation of dispositions in at least the seminal Prior, Pargetter and Jackson (1982) and by Armstrong (1997)[28]. This "carrier thesis", as Brüntrup (2016, p. 52) calls it, has its earliest predecessor already in Aristotle's hylomorphic duality between form and prime matter, and has been repeated in the history of philosophy by at least Leibniz and Kant[29]. But the fact remains that, from the point of view of purely empirical, third-person science, we have no reason to think that *anything* has an intrinsic nature, or that any intrinsic properties exist.

Still, there is another datum that does seem to give us

---

[28] Prior, Pargetter and Jackson argue roughly that since the manifestation of any disposition D can be mimicked by certain external conditions without being intuitively a true manifestation of D, the disposition D must have some intrinsic property or complex of properties to act as the causal basis for its true manifestation. Armstrong argues for intrinsic (categorical) properties by way of their being required to act as the truth-makers for counterfactual dispositions, i.e. dispositions that have no factual manifestation, but that would have were certain conditions to occur (p. 79).

[29] An argument similar to the argument from intrinsic natures was offered by Kant in the Critique of Pure Reason, where he argues that we are cognizant of the things of the world of phenomena (here used in the Kantian sense) only "through forces operative in it", that is, through its relational and dispositional structure; but that these relations "must have internal determinations and forces", that is, intrinsic, noumenal properties. These noumenal properties he muses, with the panpsychist, to be "something which is either itself thought or something analogous to it". Kant immediately afterwards refers to Leibniz and how he, too, found that the "subjective property of sensibility" must antecede the apparent world of matter, "[making] experience itself possible". (1782/2003, pp. 171–172). Leibniz offered many arguments for the existence of intrinsic properties in his writings, one of which concerns his observation that substance must be ontologically prior to extension, since extension is merely the repetition of substance—and that therefore extension cannot be the complete nature of concrete reality, needing an intrinsic base that is extended (McDonough, 2014).

epistemic access to the intrinsic nature of a physical object: our experience of ourselves, our own consciousness. In our own particular case it does seem like there are such things as intrinsic properties, these being the *qualia* discussed in chapter 1.1. We are complex physical objects—indeed, only physical if a physicalist monist doctrine is adhered to—and in our case we have an intrinsic nature, and this intrinsic nature is phenomenal. As Seager (2006 p. 142) writes, the existence of our first-person experience of being ourselves is our best evidence for the existence of any kind of intrinsic property—and since empirical, third-person science cannot even in principle access this epistemic datum of *being something* instead of merely *observing something*, phenomenality remains to it utterly alien and mysterious.

So we have only one instance of access to what the intrinsic nature of a physical object is, and in this case that intrinsic nature is phenomenal. It is here that the argument begins to turn in favor of panpsychism as an explanatory doctrine. Panpsychism postulates that all physical things have an intrinsic side to them, and that like in our own case, this intrinsic nature is phenomenal. Though there is not—and in principle cannot be—any empirically verifiable evidence for ubiquitous phenomenality, such a postulation arguably gains much theoretical merit from its simplicity and parsimony. Anti-panpsychist physicalism has to postulate at least two, and possibly three fundamentally different kinds of intrinsic natures to concretely existing objects: experiential, as in our own case; non-experiential in the case of non-conscious, 'merely physical' nature; and, possibly, non-existing, in case it is argued that only conscious beings have intrinsic natures at all, and only a limited range of objects (such as people, animals, or more widely biological organisms) count as conscious beings. In comparison, panpsychism requires only one fundamental category of intrinsic natures, the experiential.

CHAPTER TWO

Though it postulates a vastly larger number of intrinsic natures and properties than, for example, the relations-only metaphysics of Ladyman et al. (2007), it need not postulate several categories of them, making it arguably theoretically more parsimonious. Philip Goff calls this the *argument from simplicity* for panpsychism (e.g. Goff 2017b). Panpsychism makes the intrinsic natures of the micro- and the macrolevel continuous with each other. The microphenomenal *just is* the microphysical, simply seen from the point of view of its intrinsic nature instead of its extrinsic nature.

Furthermore, once we take again into account the fact that physics and the other empirical sciences cannot even in principle have anything to say about what exactly a non-experiential intrinsic nature would be, we are struck by how large a theoretical commitment such a postulation would be. To cite Strawson at length:

> One of the most important experiences that a philosopher brought up in the (recent) Western tradition can undergo is the realization that [there is no good reason to believe that anything nonexperiential exists]: the belief in irreducibly non-experiential reality has no respectable foundation, even given a fully realist commitment to belief in an external world of tables and chairs. A world that exists wholly independently of one's own mind and one's experiences— and a conviction that physics and cosmology– and indeed the other sciences—get a very great deal right about the nature and structure of reality. (2016 p. 98).

It is thus the case that the very existence of anything intrinsically non-experiential is a wholly pre-scientific and pre-empirical intuition, lacking any sort of theoretical or evidential support. Here the "incredulous stare" against panpsychism gets turned on its head: instead of demanding evidence for the ludicrousness of ubiquitous experientiality, we are shocked by the complete lack of evidence for anything non-experiential. We can thus see two sides in the argument from intrinsic natures or the argument from simplicity: the positive, which observes that we have direct evidence—indeed, the most direct evidence possible—that at least some objects are intrinsically experiential, and that in the name of parsimony we should postulate the same kind of intrinsic existence to other objects as well; and the negative, which observes that there is, in contrast, no evidence whatsoever that any object is intrinsically non-experiential. Physicalism in the sense defined above requires, if it aims to respect the Consciousness Constraint, a commitment to radical (or super-strong) emergence as defined above in chapter 2.3.

2.6 Conclusion

We have now argued for the theoretical inferiority of classical physicalism as compared to panpsychism, taking into account the emergence problem, the conceivability argument, and the argument from intrinsic natures. The next step is to elucidate the alternative, panpsychism. The latter theory faces its own problems, however, of which the most pressing (and discussed) one is the combination problem. In the upcoming chapters we shall first go over some variants of panpsychism as well as the combination problem in its several forms, and see how the many different panpsychisms fare against the challenge of the problem.

CHAPTER THREE

THE VARIETIES OF PANPSYCHISM

3.1 Defining Panpsychism

It is only now, after our discussion of physicalism, fundamentality, and grounding, that we have the tools in hand to finally give a reasonable definition of panpsychism itself:

> *Panpsychism:* The thesis that the entities that act as the *fundamental, grounding base* of *concrete reality* either 1) are by their *intrinsic nature* phenomenally conscious, experiential entities; or 2) somehow involve phenomenal or experiential processes, have a conscious or experiential aspect[30] to them, or have phenomenal or experiential properties.

The core of panpsychism is, then, the fundamentality of phenomenality, that it is not grounded by or reducible by analysis to the objects and descriptions of theoretical physics.

However, within this umbrella concept of panpsychism there are a plethora of conceptually possible variations. The above

---

[30] Where "aspect" is taken to be, following Goff (2017a, pp. 225-227), a structural constituent or element of any kind of a larger whole under which it is subsumed.

definition itself points out an important distinction. The first clause of the disjunction refers to a property monist type of panpsychism, where concretely existing entities are by their intrinsic nature wholly phenomenal. The second clause of the disjunction refers to a property dualist or dual aspect type of panpsychism, where concretely existing entities are by their intrinsic nature in part constituted by phenomenal properties and in part by non-phenomenal properties. I am sufficiently convinced by the arguments of Strawson (2006a, 2016) about the inevitable collapse of property dualism to substance dualism[31] to discount it as a viable option, and shall thus concentrate on the property monist versions of panpsychism.

We shall next advance to survey the prime varieties of panpsychism, doing this via three relevant distinctions[32]: first, the distinction between constitutive and non-constitutive (emergent) panpsychism; second, the distinction between panpsychism and panprotopsychism; and third, a distinction within constitutive panpsychism between smallist/fundamentalist panpsychism and priority cosmopsychist panpsychism.

3.2 Constitutive and Non-constitutive Panpsychism

The first important distinction within property monist panpsychism in turn is that between *constitutive* and *non-constitutive*

---

[31] Strawson's argument is, in a nutshell, that no entity X can possess both fundamental and intrinsic experiential properties and fundamental and intrinsic non-experiential properties without being factorable into separate portions, one being wholly experiential and the other wholly non-experiential. The argument turns on the idea that such a property dualism would require an additional quiddity on top of the properties themselves, which would carry both types of properties and act as a kind of a 'mixing base'. In Strawson's view, with which I agree, no such quiddity can be found on top of the intrinsic properties themselves.

[32] Goff (2017a) categorizes the varieties of panpsychism using these same three dimensions (p. 19).

CHAPTER THREE

panpsychism. In the constitutive forms of panpsychism, the macrophenomenal is seen to be constituted by the microphenomenal, formed by the microphenomenal; macrophenomenal subjects by microphenomenal subjects, macrophenomenal properties by microphenomenal properties, and so on. The microphenomenal is seen as the fundamental grounding base of the macrophenomenal. Most commonly the idea in constitutive panpsychism is that whatever entities are the ultimate, fundamental grounding base of physical facts (elementary particles, for example), the intrinsic natures (or quiddities) of those entities are phenomenal in nature; and that just as those microphysical particles and processes combine to form macrophysical objects and events, they equally combine to form macrophenomenal objects and events. In other words, the constitutive panpsychist might claim that the consciousness of a human being is literally built from smaller consciousnesses, eventually those of the elementary particles.

In non-constitutive forms of panpsychism, no such clear-cut combinatorial relation is seen to hold between the microphenomenal and the macrophenomenal. One such alternative to constitutivism is emergentism, where the macrophenomenal is itself seen as fundamental. In other words, in non-constitutive panpsychism, macrophenomenal phenomena such as human and animal subjective consciousnesses are themselves fundamental and ungrounded in facts about their "smaller" constituents or some otherwise more fundamental facts. This is often presented in the form of a strong emergence of the macrophenomenal from the microphenomenal (for an explanation of strong emergence, see chapter 2.3. above). There are two major forms of emergent panpsychism in the literature: synchronic and diachronic. The first of these treats the phenomenal as organized into separate, equally fundamental layers, postulating both a layer of fundamental microphenomenality as well as a layer of fundamental macrophenomenality, which are ungrounded in each other but exist synchronically (i.e. simultaneously). The synchronic emergent forms of panpsychism are often criticized for not quite fulfilling the monist ideal of constitutive panpsychism, as well as for potentially inheriting some of the most severe problems of dualism, especially the problem of mental or macrophenomenal causation and the resulting dilemma of epiphenomenalism and systematic causal overdetermination (e.g. Chalmers 2016a, p. 30), discussed above in chapter 2.3.

Another synchronic (yet not quite emergentist) form of non-constitutive panpsychism is what Chalmers (2016b) calls *identity panpsychism*, where the macrophenomenal is seen as identical to a particular microphenomenal entity, event or property. Identity panpsychism has some affinity with Leibnizian *monadology*, where the human soul is considered the dominant monad in a system of countless other monads, all of which are, though qualitatively different due to each monad's unique degree of likeness to the perfection of God, essentially similar in the sense of being subjects with perceptive faculties (Leibniz 1714/2017). In identity panpsychism, the macrosubject (such as a person) is identical with one of the countless microsubjects making it up, such as a single quark, which just happens to be the dominant macrosubject by chance. The obvious problems with this view concern the stability and causal powers of that single microsubject: What happens to the macrosubject when the relatively short-lived quark disappears or is annihilated? And how on Earth could it possess the kind of causal powers we would like to attribute to the macrosubject? Its causal powers can hardly be identical to those it possesses from the empirical point of view of its extrinsic properties, as those are arguably quite limited[33]—or

---

[33] At the very least there should be empirical evidence that a single particle, such as a quark, could hold such a systemically relevant, dominant and interconnected role in a system such as the human nervous system. I am quite sure there is no such evidence, though the proviso must be given that there might not be any logical inconsistency in the idea.

otherwise we again face (relative) epiphenomenalism. Identity panpsychism thus has great trouble incorporating the causal efficacy of the macrophenomenal.

There is a third option, situated conceptually somewhat between synchronic emergent panpsychism and identity panpsychism: *diachronic emergent panpsychism*. Diachronic emergent panpsychism seems currently to be the most promising version of emergent panpsychism, exemplified by *panpsychist infusion* as spearheaded by William Seager (2010, 2016). The gist of panpsychist infusion is that, though there is an ubiquitous and fundamental layer of microphenomenal entities corresponding to the intrinsic side of microphysical entities, in certain conditions and according to certain laws of *combinatorial infusion*, these entities fuse together to form macrophenomenal entities in such a manner that the microphenomenal and microphysical entities cease to exist—they permanently contribute their individual existence to the resultant macro-entity. Hence, the emergence is diachronic (i.e. non-simultaneous): first the microphenomenal entities exist as individual and separate entities, but after their organization fulfils certain conditions, the microphenomenal layer is completely wiped out, and the macrophenomenal comes into being[34]. Panpsychist infusion will be considered further in chapter 5.1.1; suffice it here to say that it also suffers from problems of mental causation, especially if we want to adhere to the principle of the causal closure of the physical.

For the constitutive panpsychist, the causal relevance of macrophenomenal properties is directly inherited from the

---

[34] Chalmers (2016b) considers the question whether the infusion should be understood as synchronic or diachronic in nature, concluding that synchronic infusion would face significant trouble with an overproliferation of subjects, the phenomenal counterpart to the problem of the many (pp. 198–200). The diachronic nature of infusion is already made explicit in Seager (2010) for the same reasons (p. 181).

microphenomenal, which is seen as identical to the microphysical. The causal powers of the macrophenomenal function by way of the microphenomenal. The emergent panpsychist does not have recourse to the same answer. Since the macrophenomenal is not grounded in the microphenomenal, it is at the very least difficult to see how it could inherit the causal relevance of the latter.

The core similarity between all forms of non-constitutive panpsychism (or at the very least those considered here) is that they consider the macrophenomenal itself as fundamental. The emergent panpsychists, both synchronic and diachronic, could say that the macrophenomenal is identical to the macrophysical, and that the macrophenomenal is causally relevant in the same way that the macrophysical is causally relevant. But the causal relevance of the macrophysical is arguably such in virtue of the causal relevance of the microphysical, of which it is composed[35]; and if the macrophenomenal is not similarly composed of the microphenomenal, but strongly emergent from it, be it synchronically or diachronically, both its identity to the macrophysical and its causal relevance are suspect. The identity panpsychist fares not much better, since in identity panpsychism the macrophenomenal, identical to the microphenomenal, is explicitly not seen as identical to the macrophysical[36]. But despite these problems, non-constitutive panpsychism remains a valuable avenue of exploration, and does have its own proponents.

---

[35] This naturally holds only in so called smallist frameworks, as opposed to priority monist frameworks. This distinction is expounded upon below in 3.3.

[36] It might be remotely possible to form a framework where the macrophysical is equally seen as identical to the microphysical, or perhaps more realisticallya framework of mereological nihilism as concerns the macrophysical. Either option might offer the identity panpsychist some avenue for response.

CHAPTER THREE

3.3 Panpsychism and Panprotopsychism

Another major distinction, already appearing in Chalmers (1996), is one between panpsychism and *panprotopsychism*. Panpsychism itself usually postulates that, even at the most fundamental, elementary level, the intrinsic, deep, categorical nature of concrete physical matter is phenomenality or experience. In panprotopsychism, however, these elementary quiddities are merely *protophenomenal* in nature; where something is protophenomenal if it is not itself phenomenal, but is somehow something that can act so as to constitute something phenomenal or act as the emergence base for something phenomenal. Protophenomenal properties are not phenomenal, but something "close enough" that they can combine to form phenomenal properties. This is crucially not to say that any material properties, taken in the traditional, purely non-phenomenal or non-conscious sense, would count as candidates for protophenomenal properties. Chalmers (2016a) defines protophenomenal properties as "special properties with an especially close connection to phenomenal properties", and gives them two necessary criteria: first, that they are distinct from purely structural, relational or dispositional properties; and second, that there is an *a priori* entailment from truths about the protophenomenal properties to truths about the phenomenal properties they constitute (p. 31). This definition thereby excludes narrowly physical properties from being candidates for the protophenomenal base.

The principal problem for panprotopsychism is its nebulousness. As Goff (2017a) argues, the definition of protophenomenality is partly indirect and partly *via negativa*—protophenomenal properties are those properties that are *not* phenomenal, though *neither* structural. They are the quiddities of concrete entities, and they *somehow* give rise to the phenomenal, but how this happens and what their actual nature is remains essentially unknown, and seemingly unknowable, noumenal. (ibid. pp. 166–167). How big of a problem this nebulousness is, however, is a matter of opinion. Many philosophers[37] and scientists[38] have argued that the cognitive capacities of the human mind might simply be limited to such a degree that a thorough understanding of the genesis of phenomenal consciousness is impossible, a viewpoint dubbed *new mysterianism,* following Owen Flanagan (1991). From this point of view there is no additional theoretical disadvantage in nebulousness or noumenalism. Goff (2017a) further argues that even though no positive conception of protophenomenality is available to us currently, this is not to prove that such a conception remains impossible in principle (p. 168). Taking these considerations into account, panprotopsychism remains a conceptually possible alternative. The most influential modern panprotopsychist theory is the Panqualityism of Sam Coleman (e.g. 2014, 2016), which postulates phenomenal qualities to be only protopsychist phenomena, lacking in themselves any subjectivity. The core idea is then essentially that phenomenal qualities can exist without being experienced by anyone—and that only in particular configurations are they linked together in such a way that a subject is formed, to whom they are then presented. A more in-depth overview of panqualityism remains, unfortunately, outside the scope of the current work. But the view is certainly interesting, and deeply rooted in the history of panpsychism in the

---

[37] James (1896) argued for the limitations of human understanding as comes to the functioning of the human mind. Colin McGinn (1989, 2006) is perhaps the foremost contemporary proponent of this view. At the same time it has to be said that though James was arguably quite favourable towards pan(proto)psychistic theories, McGinn (2006) famously discounts the panpsychistic project as "utter balderdash… vaguely hippyish, i.e. stoned" (p. 93). Whether this can be considered a proper argument is naturally questionable.

[38] The renowned cognitive psychologist Steven Pinker (2007) promotes the view that the human brain is limited in its cognitive capacity in such a way that it simply cannot grasp the genesis of consciousness.

thought of such writers as Ernst Mach (see e.g. 1883/1942) and Herbert Feigl (e.g. 1960), among others.

3.4 Smallism and Priority Cosmopsychism

A third important distinction, primarily within the field of constitutive panpsychism, is between *smallist* or *fundamentalist*[39] panpsychism and *priority cosmopsychist* panpsychism. Smallist panpsychism considers the microphenomenal intrinsic natures of whatever are the ultimate, atomic, non-composite microphysical entities, such as elementary particles, as the fundamental, grounding base of the macrophenomenal. This has traditionally been the received form of panpsychism: that even the smallest particles of matter have a phenomenal intrinsic nature, and that these combine or in some other way act so as to form macrophenomenal entities. Smallism thus mirrors the received popular image of physics, which sees the microphysical as the fundamental grounding base of the macrophysical.

Though smallism is arguably both the received view both in philosophy as well as the popular imagination, the alternative of *priority monism* has gained some ground in recent decades, especially following Jonathan Schaffer's (e.g. 2003, 2010) advocacy of the view. Priority monism, in general, postulates that all the apparently myriad objects and properties of concrete reality are grounded, not in the existence and properties of a legion of fundamental, non-composite simples, but in the

---

[39] The term "smallism" originates, to my knowledge, in Coleman (2006), where he uses the term to characterize the background assumptions of Strawson's (2006a) critique of emergentism. "Fundamentalism" is used in a way quite synonymous to smallism by Montero (2006) and Nagasawa and Wager (2016). Smallism seems to me to have gained more prominence, being the term of choice for e.g. Goff (2017a). It also avoids confusion, since cosmopsychism also refers to a fundamental level of reality, though at the cosmic instead of the micro level.

existence and properties of the entirety of the cosmos. In priority monism, there is only one fundamental object, the cosmos itself; thus it is called monism. The one fundamental object is, as the only fundamental object, metaphysically prior to everything else; thus it is called *priority* monism. The cosmos itself is infinitely decomposable into metaphysically secondary parts.

Priority cosmopsychism, defended in one form or another by at least Shani (2015), Nagasawa & Wager (2016), Goff (2017a, pp. 220–255), and Shani & Keppler (2018), is basically the idea of priority monism applied in the context of phenomenality: the phenomenality of humans, animals and other macrophenomenal entities is grounded not in the microphenomenal, but instead in the *cosmophenomenal,* the phenomenality of the cosmos as a whole. As in the case of the microphenomenal in more smallist varieties of panpsychism, so also in cosmopsychism the phenomenality of the cosmos is not necessarily to be understood to be in any way equivalent to the robust phenomenality of humans. Even though the cosmos is literally 'bigger' than a human organism, this does not mean that its phenomenality must correspondingly be more sophisticated and variegated. Though priority cosmopsychism (and, perhaps to a lesser degree, priority monism in general) may feel counterintuitive and estranged from a scientific worldview, it's a logically and conceptually coherent view which could possibly help solve some of the most serious problems facing panpsychism, as we will see in chapter 5.2.2.

The three distinctions or axes considered here are by themselves not enough to represent the entire variety of panpsychist or closely related theories. Their purpose, for now, is to shed some light on the field of panpsychism, though not nearly entirely illuminating it. We shall next move on to present the most discussed and most severe problem concerning panpsychism, the combination problem, and eventually how the many panpsychisms can answer its challenge.

CHAPTER FOUR

THE COMBINATION PROBLEM

The term *combination problem* originates in Seager (1995), but the problem itself is older[40], and is often seen to have had its most influential early formulation in William James (1890/1951), where he presents an argument against the combination of mental states in what he termed *mind dust* theories, roughly the 19th century equivalents of modern panpsychism. I cite James here at length:

> Take a hundred of them [feelings], shuffle them and pack them as close together as you can (whatever that may mean); still each remains the same feeling it always was, shut in its own skin, windowless, ignorant of what the other feelings are and mean. There would be a hundred-and-first feeling there, if, when a group or series of such feelings were set up, a consciousness belonging to the group as such should emerge. And this 101st feeling would be a totally new fact; the 100 original feelings might, by a curious physical law, be a signal for its creation, when they came together; but they would have no substantial identity with it, nor it with them, and one

---

[40] The problem was raised and considered in brief by at least Leibniz, Kant, and Diderot well before James, though James is the most cited example. (Skrbina 2011, p. 123).

could never deduce the one from the others, or (in any intelligible sense) say that they evolved it. (p. 160)

Though this passage of James is actually part of a larger argument against any type of composition or combination, including that of physical objects[41], the mental subtype has had more of an influence on its own in contemporary literature. The combination problem, at its most simple, is therefore the question of how exactly phenomenal qualities and subjects can merge together to form the macrophenomenal qualities and subjects we are familiar with—ourselves and our experiences.

In contemporary literature, the combination problem appears in the form of three separate sub-problems. This taxonomy of the problem originates Chalmers (2016b) and is widely applied in current debate as the standard representation of the problem therein: it appears as such in at least Goff (2017a), Goff et al. (2017), Strawson (2016) and Coleman (2016). The sub-problems are the *subject-summing problem*, having to do with how separate subjects can combine to form larger or more robust macrosubjects; the *quality combination problem*, also known as the *palette problem*, having to do with how the full array of robust phenomenal complexity in human macroexperience could be constituted by a very limited amount of different phenomenal simples, such as the intrinsic properties of microphysical objects; and the *structural mismatch problem*, also called the *grain problem*, having to do with a seeming structural disparity between the macrophysical (e.g. the brain, as revealed to us through empirical science) and the macrophenomenal (e.g. human macroexperience).

---

[41] "[N]o possible number of entities (call them as you like, whether forces, material particles, or mental elements) can sum themselves together... The "water" is just the old atoms in the new position, H-O-H..." (p. 159).

CHAPTER THREE

I shall next advance to describe each of these sub-problems in more detail, starting with the subject-summing problem. Since non-constitutive panpsychism does not imply that the macrophenomenal, be it qualities, entities or processes, is constituted by the microphenomenal, and instead takes it as fundamental, it avoids some of the problems having to do with actual combination as well as grounding. Emergent forms of panpsychism do face the question of which conditions are adequate for the emergence of a macrophenomenal entity; for example, what are the actual laws of combinatorial infusion in diachronic emergent infusion theories, considered in more detail below in 5.1.1.

4.1 The Subject-Summing Problem

The basic form of the subject-summing problem[42] is one of a conceivability argument, much like the one we saw reared against physicalism in chapter 2.4. The general idea is that whatever microphenomenal subjects constitute the kind of macrophenomenal subject involved in human macroexperience, it seems conceivable that all those microphenomenal subjects could exist without the macrophenomenal subject existing. Though we cannot conceive of the constituent bricks of a building existing in the same arrangement without the building simultaneously coming to exist, the idea is that the same does not apply to distinct subjects—paraphrasing James, no matter how close you pack two of them, it's still conceivable that they do not form a third further subject. Goff (2017a, p. 174) expresses this idea in the following principle:

> *Conceivable Isolation of Subjects (CIS):* For any group of subjects, $S_1, S_2 \ldots S_n$, and any conscious states, $E_1, E_2 \ldots E_n$, the following scenario is conceivable: there are $S_1, S_2 \ldots S_n$ instantiating $E_1, E_2 \ldots E_n$ respectively, but

---
[42] The term originates in Goff (2009).

it's not the case that there is a subject S* such that S* is not identical with any of $S_1, S_2 \ldots S_n$.

In other words, CIS states that no matter what conscious states any arbitrary set of subjects instantiate, it is conceivable that they do not form any further, novel macrosubject. If we further believe the conceivability principle as it was reared against the physicalist in chapter 2.4—that, at the very least as comes to phenomenal properties, conceivability entails possibility—this conceivability seems to entail its metaphysical possibility, leading to the following modal principle (ibid., 176):

Modal Isolation of Subjects (MIS): For any group of subjects, $S_1, S_2 \ldots S_n$, and any conscious states, $E_1, E_2 \ldots E_n$, the following scenario is possible: there are $S_1, S_2 \ldots S_n$ instantiating $E_1, E_2 \ldots E_n$ respectively, but it's not the case that there is a subject S* such that S* is not identical with any of $S_1, S_2 \ldots S_n$.

Since grounding demands logical entailment from the more to the less fundamental, as we saw above in chapter 2.2, and since (smallist) constitutive panpsychism is exactly the thesis that the microphenomenal grounds by analysis the macrophenomenal, the microphenomenal should logically entail the macrophenomenal—that is, in any case where a macrosubject is constituted by a group of microsubjects, it should not be possible that the latter group exists without the former also existing—and thus MIS cannot hold simultaneously with (smallist) constitutive panpsychism [43].

---

[43] This step to a modal principle, though taken here, might not in the end be necessary. This is because constitutive panpsychism already commits to the position that the relationship between micro- and macrophenomenality is intelligible and understandable, and hence the negation of the constitution should not be conceivable. (Goff 2017a, p. 176)

CHAPTER FOUR

All attempts to counter the subject-summing problem (or indeed the subject irreducibility problem) must therefore answer the question of how exactly subjects can intelligibly sum. A satisfactory suggestion for a combinatory relation, law or mechanism must be such that the conjunction of all facts about the microphenomenal, in conjunction with the posited combinatory relation, law or mechanism, makes it unintelligible that the microphenomenal facts about, say, the constituents of a human being could hold without the macrophenomenal facts concerning that human holding as well. In other words, any satisfactory counter to the subject-summing problem has to make *microphenomenal zombies*—beings which share all the microphysical *and* the microphenomenal properties of their conscious counterparts, without instantiating any macrophenomenal properties—inconceivable.

At the same time any counter to the subject-summing problem must find its own balance between an overproliferation of subjects on one hand, which comes about when the criteria for subject-summing are particularly loose, and absolute monism or the existence of only one cosmic subject on the other, which comes about when the criteria for subject-summing are particularly strict—the "Scylla and Charybdis" of subject-summing (Chalmers 2016b, p. 201).

4.2 The Quality-Combination Problem

The *quality-combination problem* has to do with how microphenomenal properties or *microqualities* can combine to form macrophenomenal properties or *macroqualities,* where the former means the phenomenal properties of whatever particles or processes form the ultimate and fundamental level of physical reality, and the latter means the specific qualities in human experience, our ordinary qualia, such as the blueness of the sky, the smell of fresh coffee etc. The difference to the subject-summing problem, as described above, is that whereas the subject-summing problem has to do with how microsubjects can combine together to constitute a novel macrosubject, the quality-combination problem has to do with how the qualia of elementary subjects could combine to form the qualia of macrosubjects. (e.g. Chalmers 2016, Goff et al. 2017a) How does this combination happen? What kind of a combination relation is in effect here?

The quality-combination problem is also called the *palette problem*. The question here is that since (ostensibly) the variety of microphysical ultimates, and thereby the variety of microqualia, is limited to perhaps a handful of different simples, how can this very limited array of qualities combine to form the vast range of macroqualities we can perceive in our experience—that is, how is it possible to paint such a vibrant and multifarious painting as the experiential life of a human being, experienced in multiple sensory modalities, with so very few colors. After all, as Goff (2017a, pp. 194–196) argues, it is unclear if there are even so many microphysical ultimates as to match our sensory modalities in number, and as the sensory modalities seem so distinct from each other, it is difficult to see how they could be formed of the same primary constituents. Chalmers (2016b, p. 189) frames this argument in the following formulation:

(1) If constitutive panpsychism is correct, macrophenomenal qualities are constituted by microphenomenal qualities.
(2) If Russellian[44] panpsychism is correct, there are only a few microphenomenal qualities.

---

[44] By Russellian panpsychism Chalmers refers to panpsychism that takes microphenomenal qualities as the quiddities or categorical bases of microphysical dispositions (2016a, p. 26). Since Russellian panpsychism is the only kind of panpsychism answering the crucial motivating questions about the intrinsic nature of the physical and the place of phenomenality in nature, I have refrained from subtyping it as a distinct variety of panpsychism elsewhere.

CHAPTER FOUR

(3) Macrophenomenal qualities are too diverse to be constituted by a few microphenomenal qualities.
(4) Constitutive Russellian panpsychism is incorrect.

The third premise is the one that should be targeted in a proper counter to the argument (unless one is again defending a non-constitutive form of panpsychism such as emergentism, which avoids the problem for the most part by committing to fundamental macroqualities). A proper counter to the quality-combination problem should thus (1) suggest a relation or mechanism by which qualities can combine to begin with and (2) explain how the ostensibly limited quantity of phenomenal simples can, through the particular combination relation suggested, be adequate to form the rich variety of macroqualities we find in human experience.

Another serious problem having to do with quality combination as well as subject summing is the *perspective objection*, formulated originally by Sam Coleman (2014) and repeated with further explication by Shani (2015) and Albahari (2020). The perspective objection basically pivots around the idea that, since the subjective experiences, the points of view, of subjects always occur as total experiences *to the exclusion of everything else,* they can never appear subsumed as parts of a larger subjective experience. The point of view of each subject is, as it were, a total *perspective,* which is just as it is and cannot include any other. The point is thus that the qualitative contents of subjects can be such as to exclude other possible qualitative contents, rendering their simultaneous appearance in a larger mind in which they are subsumed contradictory. Goff (2017a, p. 189–191) argues that the fact that some subjective experience is subsumed in a larger whole does not mean that the former has to characterize the latter, i.e. appear as such as part of the larger experience. Although I believe that Goff's counter does have some force, I have in this work given the benefit of the doubt in favor of the perspective objection, and will consider it here on the assumption of its veracity.

4.3 The Structural Mismatch Problem

The *structural mismatch problem* concerns a seeming mismatch between the macrophysical strucutre as revealed to us through the natural sciences and empirical observation, and the macrophenomenal structure as it appears in our experience (e.g. Chalmers 2016b, Goff et al. 2017). The idea is that, since in a true property monist panpsychism the microphysical and the microphenomenal properties of fundamental objects or processes (be they the quarks and leptons of current theoretical physics or something else) are identical, they should naturally be *isomorphic*[45] to each other. Then, since at the micro-level the microphysical and the microphenomenal are isomorphic, the microphenomenal constitutes the macrophenomenal, and the microphysical constitutes the macrophysical, the macrophysical and the macrophenomenal should also be isomorphic to each other. I once again follow Chalmers (2016a, p. 206), in providing the following formulation:

(1) If Russellian panpsychism is true, microphenomenal structure is isomorphic to microphysical structure.
(2) If constitutive panpsychism is true, microphenomenal (and microphysical) structure constitutes macrophenomenal structure.
(3) Microphysical structure constitutes only macrophysical structure.

---

[45] Isomorphism between two things means roughly that they share the same structure, though the constituents making up that structure may be different.

CHAPTER FOUR

(4) If microphenomenal structure is isomorphic to microphysical structure, then any structure constituted by microphenomenal structure (and microphysical structure) is isomoprhic to a structure constituted by microphysical structure.
(5) Macrophenomenal structure is not isomorphic to macrophysical structure.
(6) Constitutive Russellian panpsychism is false.

The premises most susceptible to attack here are the premises (4) and (5). (4) could be attacked on the grounds that though the microphysical and the microphenomenal are isomorphic, they combine in different ways to form slightly different composites, even though both composites are grounded in isomorphic bases. But this might require some kind of property dualism, since it would complicate the idea that the macrophenomenal side to a structure is the quiddity to its macrophysical side. A better counter to the structural mismatch problem should thereby, in my view, attack premise (5), and argue that the seeming disparity between the macrophenomenal and the macrophysical is only just that, a seeming disparity—and that actually if we were to understand the nature of reality better both from the physical and the phenomenal point of view, there would no longer seem to be any such disparity.

This is, then, the famed combination problem for panpsychism. The problem has loomed large in one way or the other over the panpsychist view for centuries. Yet it ought not to be taken as a fatal objection, not by any means; but rather as a *"call for details"*, as Skrbina (2011, p. 122) puts it. There are already many contemporary suggestions about how to go about solving the problem, to which I will next turn.

CHAPTER FIVE

SUGGESTED SOLUTIONS TO THE COMBINATION PROBLEM

Delivering an adequate response to the combination problem is arguably the most important and discussed topic in the field of panpsychism at present. A proper, full-fledged solution to the problem should be able to answer all the three subproblems in a satisfying and unified way. As Chalmers (2016, p. 184) writes, most of the currently available suggestions target one of the subproblems especially, but though they can manage to accommodate their focused subproblem the others keep on making trouble. I will next go through some of the suggested solutions and survey their merits and faults.

5.1 The Non-Combinatorial Response

One way to solve the problem of phenomenal combination is naturally to say that there is no phenomenal combination. This is the answer of the non-constitutive panpsychists, be they emergents or identity panpsychists: the synchronic emergentist sees the macrophenomenal as strongly emergent[46] and fundamental,

---

[46] Though not superstrongly or radically emergent, as is the case with the physicalist, since the emergence would be, though a posteriori, still intra-attributive.

CHAPTER FIVE

ungrounded in either the microphenomenal or the cosmophenomenal; whereas the identity panpsychist sees the macrophenomenal already as identical to the simple, non-composite microphenomenal. As an answer to the combination problem this is certainly very nifty—however, as we have seen, both the emergent panpsychist and the identity panpsychist face certain severe difficulties of their own. We have already gone over these in chapter 3.1 concerning constitutive and non-constitutive panpsychism, so I will not repeat them at length here—so suffice it to say that the synchronic emergent panpsychist faces, with the substance dualist, serious difficulties concerning mental causation and causal overdetermination, being thereby threatened by epiphenomenalism; whereas the identity panpsychist faces problems concerning the ephemerality of possible microphysical counterparts to the macrosubject, as well as the mismatch between the empirically observable causal powers of any possible microphysical counterpart and the macrosubject, resulting again in the threat of epiphenomenalism.

5.1.1 Panpsychist Infusion

As was mentioned in chapter 3.1, one contemporary variety of non-constitutive panpsychism does stand out in current debate. This is the panpsychist infusion of Seager (2010, 2016), also defended with some modifications by Mørch (2014). As explained in 3.1, the gist of panpsychist infusion is that, when a variety of microphenomenal entities arrange in an organization that exemplifies particular laws of combinatorial infusion, those microphenomenal entities are *fused* together to form a completely novel macrophenomenal entity. This process of infusion is such that the emergence base consisting of the microphenomenal entities ceases to exist at the moment of infusion exactly as the macrophenomenal entity comes to be. The macroentities resulting from infusion are thus what Seager calls *large simples*, which are "partless yet extended" (p. 180). The relation between the emergence base and the emergent macroentity, the relation of combinatorial infusion, is thereby diachronic (i.e. non-simultaneous) in nature.

A relevant question here is whether or not subjecthood is to be considered a *maximal* property. The concept of maximal property comes from Ted Sider (2001), who defines maximal properties as those properties which can characterize only whole objects, without characterizing any of the proper parts of those objects. Being a rock, for example, is a maximal property: only the largest possible spatially continuous sum of rock-matter is a rock. Respectively, none of the proper parts of the rock, the different areas or slices of rock-matter, is to be considered a rock. (p. 357–358). The idea here is to avoid the massive over-proliferation of rocks which would result from considering each proper part of the rock, each area of rock-matter, as well as their various combinations also as rocks.

Sider argues, however, that maximal properties are necessarily extrinsic properties: they are always dependent on other objects, hence they are relational, and hence they are extrinsic. A piece of rock-matter, for example, is a rock just in case it is not a proper part of any larger continuous area of rock-matter—the property of being a rock is dependent on whether or not the object is a part of a larger object (ibid. p. 360). Sider (2003) further argues that to avoid a massive over-proliferation of subjects, the property of subjecthood must be considered a maximal property—and since maximal properties are by necessity extrinsic, subjecthood must also be an extrinsic property (p. 145). This result, though acceptable to Sider (2003, p. 149) naturally contradicts the arguably intuitive view that a psychophysical duplicate of a phenomenally conscious being would share the phenomenal properties of the original. Since intrinsic properties should survive such duplication, this also eliminates our only plausible access to the intrinsic properties of anything. Though this might be a positive result for those endorsing ontologies of mere structure, it is well worth the effort for the panpsychist to try to find some other answer to the conundrum.

In contrast, Seager (2010) disagrees that subjecthood and phenomenal properties should be considered maximal, defining them instead as *aggregative*: as non-maximal properties which are also shared by all the proper parts of an object, and which, in the case of the whole object, become a kind of an aggregate or sum of the similar properties of all the parts of the object. Seager gives mass as an example of an aggregative property: the proper parts of any object that has mass also have mass, and the mass of the whole object is the sum of the masses of its parts[47]. Though all the proper parts of any ordinary massive object, such as a rock, have mass themselves, when they are parts of the rock as a whole object their individual masses are in a sense subsumed or infused into the mass of the whole object. There is no double counting; there is not the mass of the rock as a whole, plus the masses of all of its parts. When the parts are integrated in an object, their many masses sum to become the mass of the single object.

The crux of Seager's infusionism, then, is that the property of being a conscious being, or the property of subjecthood, ought to be considered an aggregative property in the same way as mass. Although there exists a ubiquitous layer of microphenomenality corresponding to the intrinsic side of the microphysical, when these microphenomenal objects fuse together to become a macrophenomenal entity, their individual consciousnesses and phenomenal properties should no longer be doubly counted in addition to the consciousness and phenomenality of the whole

---

[47] However, as Seager also points out, this is a simplification: mass does not, in reality, add up in quite such a straightforward manner.

object (e.g. a human) of which they are part. This answer would respect Sider's argument about the necessary extrinsicality of maximal properties while allowing consciousness and phenomenal properties to be intrinsic, without implying a massive over-proliferation of subjects in the sense of the problem of the many.

However, it can be questioned whether the case of subjecthood is actually so directly comparable to that of mass. Mass is arguably not an essential property of a massive object, whereas subjecthood could be considered, especially in a panpsychist monist framework, to be the quintessential property of any object partaking of subjecthood. The proper parts of a massive object, though contributing the total of their own mass to the sum of mass of the whole object, could feasibly still continue to exist as individual parts in some other sense—whereas the microphenomenal consciousnesses fusing together into a macrophenomenal consciousness cease altogether to exist, both as microphenomenal and as microphysical entities. A counter to infusion could thereby claim that this kind of totality of contribution of the emergence base to the emergent entity is unfeasible, or at the very least outlandish.

Seager (2010, 2016) points out that there does exist already in physics examples of this kind of complete merging. Quantum entanglement is arguably a process where the entangled elementary particles (or whatever they may in the final count be) lose their individuality completely, becoming so fundamentally entwined as to count as an entirely new entity, featuring holistic properties not reducible to the entangled particles. (2010, p. 179). Quantum superposition could be considered another example of similar holism in quantum physics, where two or more bosons occupy the same quantum state, becoming completely indiscernible from each other. As Chalmers (2016b, p. 196) points out, this kind of *quantum holism,* a view that points to holistic

CHAPTER FIVE

phenomena in quantum physics to explain consciousness, holds sway outside of the field of panpsychist infusion as well. The kinds of emergence in question here are, again, diachronic in nature: the fusing particles, making up the emergence base, lose their separate identities completely, ceasing to exist while the novel, emergent entity comes to be. The idea then is that the entities resulting from such fusing together of particles in entanglement or superposition, with their novel properties, are themselves fundamental entities, irreducible and ungroundable to the fused individual particles and their relations.

One difficulty Chalmers recognizes in quantum holism is that, at least according to our current physical and neurophysiological understanding, there does not occur such stable system-wide entanglement or superposition in the human nervous system as to satisfyingly account for consciousness. Another worry is that the nature of these phenomena is still up to constant debate even within the field of physics. For example, according to some interpretations the locus of quantum entanglement is the whole universe (which would discount all varieties of quantum holism save for cosmopsychical quantum holism), whereas according to others it is either a hugely unstable phenomenon with continuous disruptions, or that it does not even occur at all—again, the Scylla and Charybdis of subject-summing. (ibid., p. 196).

In his discussion of panpsychist infusion, Chalmers (ibid., p. 199) ends up categorizing it as a form of quantum holism, and states that it inherits the problems of quantum holism explained above. Seager (2010, pp. 180–181) does point out a further example already from classical physics that is modeled in much the way that phenomenal infusion would require, the classical black hole. However, the analogy of the black hole can even at best constitute an analogy; it seems empirically quite obvious that the mechanics of black hole formation do not take place in the human nervous system—the brain is evidently not a black hole. Furthermore, as Goff (2017a, p. 152) writes, Seager's infusion theory entails that the brain, seen as identical to the fundamental, emergent macrophenomenal subject, also has no proper parts—its microphysical parts, identical with the microphenomenal parts which fuse together to form the macrophenomenal subject, cease to be upon the moment of infusion. Seager recognizes some of these difficulties, admitting that there is "little evidence that the brain supports any processes that could count as combinatorial infusion at the physical level" (p. 181).

Now that we have explicated the general merits and demerits of Seager's infusionism, let us tally the score and see how it fares against the subproblems of the combination problem. First of all, the subject-summing problem. The gist of the subject-summing problem was the following conceivability principle:

> *Conceivable Isolation of Subjects (CIS):* For any group of subjects, $S_1, S_2 \ldots S_n$, and any conscious states, $E_1, E_2 \ldots E_n$, the following scenario is conceivable: there are $S_1, S_2 \ldots S_n$ instantiating $E_1, E_2 \ldots E_n$ respectively, but it's not the case that there is a subject S^* such that S^* is not identical with any of $S_1, S_2 \ldots S_n$.

The infusionist has two avenues of defense here: the first is to deny CIS altogether, and the second is to agree only to a synchronic interpretation of CIS. The first response is the one advocated by Seager. He presents infusion as a relation of intelligible, causational emergence, stating that the conjunction of all the microphenomenal facts plus whatever are the ultimate laws of combinatorial infusion taken together imply, by logical necessity, all the macrophenomenal facts. This would mean that CIS holds only in cases where the laws of combinatorial infusion are not taken into account; and these laws, like the laws of

CHAPTER FIVE

physics, Seager considers contingent and *a posteriori*[48] (2016, p. 243). Accordingly, microphenomenal zombies would be inconceivable when the laws are taken into account. The natural question here is then how could such *a posteriori* laws be discovered, through what mechanism or method of investigation. As far as I am aware, Seager has not addressed this question as of yet, a silence which could be understood as a dismissal of the question—perhaps, for Seager it does not matter what the actual laws of combination are, just that the existence of such laws is conceptually coherent. This would amount to a type of mysterianism, in which phenomenal combination, though intelligible *in principle*, would remain, in its details, ultimately mysterious.

The second possible response would be to agree that CIS holds, but only with the slight specification that the principle is synchronic in nature—that it is conceivable that any subjects S_1, S_2 ... S_n could exist at a particular time T without any further subject existing at that same time T. Infusion is diachronic, so this synchronic reading of CIS would not apply to instances of infusion. However, it remains unclear what kind of fine difference in intuition would apply between a synchronic and a diachronic interpretation of the principle, if not exactly the addition of the diachronic laws of infusion considered above as the first avenue of response to CIS. In conclusion, Seager's infusionism does manage to give an answer to the subject-summing problem, but with the seeming cost of a commitment to mysterianism, at least until the question of how the laws of combinatorial infusion could be brought within our epistemic grasp is answered.

---

[48] This functions as a response to Chalmers' (2016b, p. 188–189) 'phenomenal' formulation of Jackson's (1982) famous knowledge argument as well. According to Seager (2016), Mary could not deduce all macrophenomenal facts even if she knows all microphysical and microphenomenal facts, but she could deduce them if, in addition, she knows all the laws of combinatorial infusion (p. 243).

PANPSYCHISM AND THE COMBINATION PROBLEM

Second, the quality combination problem. Since infusionism is a form of emergentism, the initial infusionist answer to the quality combination can be essentially very simple: since the microlayer is completely wiped out in the process of infusion, the microqualities involved in the phenomenality of the fusing microsubjects cannot in any sense constitute the macroqualities involved in the phenomenality of the resulting macrosubjects. Because there is no synchronic constitution involved, the resulting macrophenomenal qualities, which exist as novel and fundamental qualities, need not necessarily have anything in common with the previous microqualities. The diachronic emergence involved would still only be a type of strong emergence, even at the very worst, since it would in any case be an example of intra-attributive emergence. However, any strengthening of the emergence comes with the cost of a loss in intelligibility; and since Seager describes infusion as a form of intelligible emergence, this might not be a cost he would be willing to take.

If then only weak emergence is allowed, the infusionist might want to argue that the macroqualities post-infusion do in fact have something in common with the pre-infusion microqualities, and in such a way that the emergence is more or less completely intelligible if all the microqualities and the laws of combinatorial infusion are taken into account. This response ends up being essentially the same as with the subject-summing problem, and faces equally the cost of mysterianism: the emergence is completely intelligible *if* all the facts about microqualities are known and *if* the laws of combinatorial infusion are known; but once again, since the laws of combinatorial infusion seem to remain outside our epistemic grasp, the emergence remains only potentially or theoretically intelligible.

In any case, infusionism does have the benefit (as compared to the constitutive forms of panpsychism) of avoiding the perspective

CHAPTER FIVE

objection of Coleman (2014), Shani (2015) and Albahari (2020). The perspective objection, as brought up already in chapter 4.2, pivots around the idea that phenomenal qualities can be essentially such that they exist *to the exclusion* of all other qualities—that there can be, for example, a phenomenal quality the essence of which is "the experience of only redness", or "the experience of total redness", or indeed "the experience of redness to the exclusion of all other colors". The objection is then that it is impossible for the macroqualitative life of a constituted macrosubject to consist of these exclusive microqualities, since they mutually exclude each other. They cannot be *co-conscious*, that is, experienced together simultaneously by a single subject. Since the emergence in infusionism is diachronic in nature, it avoids the perspective objection as a matter of course. The microphenomenal emergence base is wiped out at the moment of infusion, and does not thereby constitute the macrophenomenal in any way. Similarly, microqualities do not constitute macroqualities, and the problem of simultaneous, exclusive and contradicting qualities does not arise.

The structural mismatch problem is the most clearly difficult one for the infusionist view. As was explained above, and as Seager himself admits, there does not, from the empirical point of view, seem to take place in the human nervous system any such process of infusion which could act as the correlate for the phenomenal infusion. An empirical correlate to infusion would have to be stable, system-wide and most importantly such that the resulting macrophysical system—which, in the panpsychistic infusionist framework, necessarily has to be isomorphic to the corresponding macrophenomenal system—is simple and thus has no proper parts. The microphysical emergence base has to cease to exist at the moment of infusion. And since the nervous system of even a living human being seems to have proper parts which can be removed or observed separately, it does not seem to fulfill these criteria.

Let's tally the score, then. Infusionism can give an answer to the subject-summing problem, but since no method of knowing the ultimate laws of combinatorial infusion is given, this only comes about at the cost of mysterianism. The same applies to the quality combination problem, unless a stronger and less intelligible form of emergence is accepted. However, infusionism does not face the perspective objection like the constitutive forms of panpsychism do. The structural mismatch problem does not seem to have any clear avenue for even a tentative answer: the macrophenomenal should be simple and fundamental, lacking any proper parts, and since the macrophenomenal and the macrophysical are isomorphic, so should the macrophysical; yet the human nervous system, which seems to, under overwhelming empirical evidence, form the macrophysical, empirical correlate to the macrophenomenal human mind, appears to indeed have proper parts.[49]

5.2 Combinatorial Responses

In contrast to non-combinatorial responses, the combinatorial responses to the combination problem do not see the macrophenomenal as fundamental. They admit of constitution

---

[49] Hedda Hassel Mørch (2014), though defending essentially a version of panpsychist infusion, differs from Seager in some regards, most crucially as comes to the totality of the infusion. In Mørch's view, microsubjects do fuse together in a diachronic process of emergence that results in the coming-to-be of novel and fundamental macrosubjects, but in such a way that the microsubjects do not cease to exist, instead becoming the non-fundamental proper parts of the novel macrosubject. Mørch's post-infusion macrosubjects can thus have non-fundamental proper parts, which are grounded in the novel macrosubject. However, this view, too, faces some serious problems: for example, the problem of how exactly would it be possible for the microsubjects that are fundamental pre-infusion to suddenly become non-fundamental post-infusion.

CHAPTER FIVE

relations between different levels of the phenomenal, as well as hierarchical grounding relations between them. Most of the constitutivist suggestions in contemporary literature are smallist in nature, committing to the view that the smaller constituents of matter and the phenomenal are the more fundamental ones; in other words, that the macrophenomenal is grounded in the microphenomenal. I shall consider one smallist framework in depth here, Phenomenal Bonding, as defended by earlier Philip Goff (2009, 2016). Smallist frameworks are not the only option, however: there is also the priority monist Priority Cosmopsychism, exemplified by Itay Shani (2015) and Yujin Nagasawa and Khai Wager (2016), lately also endorsed by Goff (2017a). Gregg Rosenberg's (2004, 2016) Theory of Natural Individuals is, due to its much more significantly revisionist nature, difficult to categorize in any pre-existing taxonomy, and serves as an example of a more unique approach to the problem. I shall next go through these suggestions in the order given above.

5.2.1 Phenomenal Bonding

Phenomenal bonding, defended at least by earlier Philip Goff (2009, 2016), is essentially the suggestion that the microphenomenal and the macrophenomenal layer coexist synchronically, i.e. there is no diachronic infusion, but that there is some kind of bonding relation which bonds all the microphenomenal subjects together so that they constitute a macrosubject. In contrast to infusion, where the microphenomenal layer is wiped out in the process of infusion and essentially replaced by the macrophenomenal layer, phenomenal bonding is closer to our ordinary sense of combination, where, for example, when a set of bricks constitute a house, the bricks still continue to exist as individual bricks even though they simultaneously constitute a larger unit as well. The idea then is that there is some kind of special relation holding between those microphenomenal entities which combine to form a larger entity, but not between those that don't. Since the framework is panpsychistic and radically monist, the relation should be such that it can also be observed empirically. Goff further suggests that this relation should preferably be fundamental in nature, and ends up choosing spatiotemporal connectivity as the most promising candidate, since our everyday notions of physical combination always or nearly always have to do with perceived spatiotemporal connectivity. (2016, p. 293–295; revisited in 2017a, p. 181–186).

However, spatiotemporal connectivity is naturally not perceived in the empirical sciences so as to be a relation of phenomenal bonding. Goff's idea here is that, similarly to how phenomenal properties act as the intrinsic natures or quiddities of physical entities, relations would also have quiddities, with the phenomenal bonding relation acting as the intrinsic nature or quiddity of spatiotemporal connectivity. The spatiotemporal relation, taken in its intrinsic guise as the phenomenal bonding relation would then be a relation of *co-consciousness:* a relation such that whenever it holds between two phenomenal states, they are experienced together in a single field of experience for a single subject.

One primary benefit of phenomenal bonding is its synchronic nature. Since there is no emergence of novel fundamental macrophenomenal entities, and the microphenomenal (and thereby the microphysical) layer is left intact, bonding theories can easily respect the principle of the causal closure of the physical. Another possible merit is their affinity with common sense conceptions of constitution, which are arguably based at least in part on spatiotemporal proximity and connectivity.

Having described the basic idea of phenomenal bonding, let us next see how it fares against the combination problem. First, the subject-summing problem. The gist of the phenomenal bonding response is essentially the same as the infusionist response. The infusionist argued that CIS, the principle of conceivable isolation of subjects, holds only when the laws of combinatorial infusion are not taken into account; in other words, that the conjunction of all microphenomenal facts and the laws of combinatorial infusion necessarily entail all macrophenomenal facts. The bonding theorist argues similarly that CIS holds only when the relation of phenomenal bonding is not taken into account; and, respectively, that the conjunction of all microphenomenal facts and the phenomenal bonding relation necessarily entail all macrophenomenal facts.

In contrast with Seager, Goff does name a clear empirically observable relation to act as the empirical counterpart to the phenomenal bonding relation: the relation of spatiotemporal connectivity. Many things other than those we would ordinarily take to be macrosubjects are spatiotemporally connected wholes, however, such as rocks, pianos and tables. To be sure, it well might be that these and all other spatiotemporally connected entities do indeed form macrosubjects; however, as Chalmers (2016b, p. 201) points out, since all spatiotemporal regions in the universe are connected, there should be some limitations to the transitivity of the phenomenal bonding relation. If the relation is wholly transitive, it seems that the view collapses into a form of cosmopsychism[50] (considered below), entailing the entire cosmos as a single, giant subject. If the relation is wholly untransitive, the phenomenal landscape becomes entirely fragmentary and we are unable to explain our ordinary human macroconsciousness. The question is then how to model the relation so that it yields our non-trivial macrosubjects, without collapsing into cosmopsychism. The phenomenal bonding theorist has their work

---

[50] In his 2017 monograph Consciousness and Fundamental Reality, Goff does indeed explicitly endorse a cosmopsychist view.

cut out for them: further criteria for what sort of spatiotemporal connectivity is meant are sorely needed. The most obvious way to go about giving such criteria would be to refer to some required level of interactional complexity between the parts of the connected object; but to do so would, again, require deep argumentation about why exactly the line is drawn there and not elsewhere. Suffice it to say that further work is needed here[51].

The bonding theorist's answer to the conceivability of microphenomenal zombies is that they are conceivable only due to our lack of understanding of the specifics of the intrinsic nature of spatiotemporal connectivity, the phenomenal bonding relation. Since the phenomenal bonding relation cannot be accessed as such by empirical observation, and its specifics do not seem to us to be introspectively obvious, the only way we could learn about them is through logical and philosophical modeling. Whatever model is ultimately given should be such that it makes microphenomenal zombies inconceivable; however, as Goff admits in his later work (2017a, p. 185–188), there is as of yet no convincing reason to suppose that such modeling is possible to the degree required. Phenomenal bonding, like infusionism, comes currently only with the cost of some level of mysterianism or noumenalism.

In terms of the quality combination problem, the phenomenal bonding theorist does not have recourse to the same answers as the

---

[51] Skrbina (2011) makes a suggestion somewhat similar to Goff's: that a configuration of particles might form a more complex unified subject when the particles "adhere sufficiently tightly, and persist together long enough" (p. 126). However, for Skrbina, subjects of consciousness (like physical objects) do not have ultimately definite limits. They instead have an "indeterminate reach" that tails off gradually into the rest of the universe. Whether this appeal to indeterminacy might help with the problems described above remains an open question worthy of further exploration. Skrbina's suggestion is somewhat evocative of "extended mind" theories of cognition and consciousness (see e.g. Telakivi, 2020), which might also make up a useful ally for the phenomenal bonding theorist.

CHAPTER FIVE

diachronic emergent infusionist. Phenomenal bonding is a synchronic and constitutive framework, and thus faces the full brunt of the quality combination problem: for it to be a complete framework, it would have to 1) explain how qualities can combine to begin with, by what mechanism and under what nomology; and 2) explain how the very limited array of possible microqualities—corresponding to the quiddities of microphysical ultimates—can, through those mechanisms and nomology, combine to form the richness and variety of human macroexperience.

Let us start with number 1, the question of how phenomenal qualities can combine. A traditional example of putative quality combination, utilized for example by Chalmers (2016b, p. 204–206), is that of colors, where it is stated that co-conscious qualities of blueness and yellowness, for example, arguably combine to form the quality of greenness. This certainly makes some sense *prima facie*. However, as Chalmers (ibid.) further points out, mere co-consciousness of the color qualities is not sufficient for them to constitute another quality, since there can be two distinct objects, one blue and one yellow, simultaneously in the visual field without any quality of greenness instantiating. Quality combination based on this example would therefore have to have some additional criteria. No such model has yet been given in the literature; a possible avenue for such a model could perhaps be to invoke some sort of phenomenal proximity, that is, the proximity of the combining qualities to each other not in the objective spatiotemporal sense of space, but in the phenomenal space of the subject's perceptual field.

At any rate, we have other reasons to doubt the self-evidence of color combination as an example of quality combination. It could be argued that the color green for example, though in the painter's everyday physical sense a mixture of blue and yellow, might as a phenomenal quality have nothing in common with the latter two colors. And even if the example of colors were to hold, do other qualities combine in the same way?

PANPSYCHISM AND THE COMBINATION PROBLEM

Some tentative evidence for the combination of at least visual qualities can be found in contemporary neuroscience. Eysenck and Keane (2010) bring forth significant evidence for at least the compositionality of visual perception, based on the finding that even highly specific subfunctions of visual perception, such as the perception of vertical lines, horizontal lines, or movement in a particular direction in the visual field, can be disrupted as a result of brain damage or repeated transcranial magnetic stimulation (rTMS). Such disruption can specifically erase only the element of horizontal extension from a subject's perception of an object, for example. From the neuroscientific point of view, visual perception consists therefore of a large variety of these subfunctions, which have their own responsibilities and neurophysiological correlates. The results of these various subfunctions are then bound together to form the final conscious perception of a coherent visual field with its distinct objects. (pp. 40–46). Although this is not yet sufficient for a proof that synchronic quality combination does indeed take place, further neuroscientific investigation might yield some suggestions as to how such combination might work.

Let us move on to the second question, the palette problem: if macroqualities consist of microqualities, and these microqualities form the quiddities of microphysical ultimates which are arguably very limited in number, how could the similarly very limited set of microqualities be a large enough palette to constitute the richness and variety of macroqualities in human experience? In particular, as Goff (2017a, pp. 194–196) argues, seeing as there are ostensibly only a handful of microphysical ultimates, qualities in different sensory modalities, such as vision and touch, would have to be at least partially built up of the same microqualitative constituents, and as they seem at least *prima facie* to be so distinct from each other, this sounds implausible.

At least three answers to the palette problem have been given in the literature as comes to constitutive versions of panpsychism.

CHAPTER FIVE

Galen Strawson (2016) takes the simplest approach and simply denies the third premise of the formalized quality combination problem (see chapter 4.2). Strawson argues that there is no palette problem: if it is possible for a handful of microphysical ultimates to create the vast variety of different objects and physical phenomena considered in the empirical sciences, it is possible for the quiddities of those ultimates to similarly create the vast variety of phenomenal qualities. After all, from an empirical point of view the sensory modalities, too, are formed from a very limited set of parameters. (p. 103). To directly quote Strawson:

> "So, too, when I consider the two groups of three parameters that account for all the colors and sounds, or the five that account for all the tastes, or the combinatorial possibilities of leptons and quarks—the astonishing variety of stuffs (lead, neurons, marshmallow) they constitute—I feel no difficulty in… the 'palette problem'." (ibid.)

Strawson's basic point is that we simply do not know enough about the physical to have sufficient reason to think that the palette problem is really a serious problem; and that perhaps our intuitions about the matter are simply mistaken.

One response that does take the palette problem to be a serious question requiring an answer is that of Coleman (2015), who argues that there might not after all be such a wide gap between the sensory modalities. There might, for example, exist a range of potential experiences that lie in between the various sensory modalities, but which are simply inaccessible to humans. Cases of synesthesia, the blending of sensory modalities together in certain mental disturbances or drug experiences, so that the experiencer reports seeing sounds or hearing color, for example, point somewhat in this direction of potential underlying unity. The fact that in our ordinary everyday consciousness the modalities are categorized so wide apart proves nothing. Coleman suggests that the variety of phenomenal qualities might not form such absolutely separate camps organized into fundamentally separate modalities, but more of a continuum which ranges over all the modalities.

Another response that takes the palette problem seriously is that of Keith Turausky (unpublished), who speculates about the nature of microphenomenality by way of analogy with light. He first considers white light, which can be taken to be a kind of undifferentiated light signal which contains, in a sense, information about all the potential colors. The other colors are, in a way, distillations or further differentiations of white light; white light filtered in a particular way, so as to remove some frequencies of light and keep others. The idea then is that the microphenomenality of elementary particles could also be in this way a still undifferentiated phenomenality, a sort of *fundamental tone* encompassing the whole of phenomenal space, which, as physical organization gets more and more complex, is filtered or refined so that only a very particular, fine slice of phenomenal space is left. The microqualities of physical ultimates would then, in a sense, already include the potentiality of all macroqualities, much like white light includes the potentiality of all colors. This would naturally eliminate the palette problem which, after all, depends on the suggested relative poverty of the microqualities as compared to macroqualities. In terms of a color palette, in Turausky's view, the microqualities are not simply an impoverished set of a few colors; instead, they are all-colored, out of which all the brilliant colors of the painting can be extracted.

Both suggestions, that of Coleman and that of Turausky, have some edge against the palette problem. The basic problem of both is that they are very speculative answers—conceptually possible suggestions which, however, have fairly little to suggest them other than the *ad hoc* motivation of solving the palette problem, especially so for Turausky's suggestion.

CHAPTER FIVE

Finally, the structural mismatch problem. Phenomenal bonding is inherently in a much better situation here than infusionism, since it does not require the bonding relation to be the kind of diachronic emergence relation which the infusionist has so much trouble finding in the empirical sciences. The bonding theorist instead postulates a synchronic relation of constitution, the bonding relation, which would be the phenomenal aspect, intrinsic nature or quiddity of an empirically observable and preferably fundamental relation. Goff's own initial suggestion for this relation, as was explained above, is the relation of spatiotemporal connectivity. But spatiotemporal connectivity is, at least in terms of the connectivity of spatiotemporal regions, an ubiquitous relation; and so, if the relation (and its quiddity, the phenomenal bonding relation) are taken to be transitive, the picture yields a single, giant, cosmic subject. If the relation is taken to be intransitive, the result is a completely fragmented phenomenal landscape with scarcely any combination at all.

There should, then, be some further specifications to what exactly the phenomenal bonding relation is. Spatiotemporal connectivity alone seems to be problematic, being either too restricting or too allowing. It is thereby relevant to consider other options, either as additional criteria on top of the spatiotemporal relation, or as entirely different answers. One answer tentatively suggested by Chalmers (2016b, p. 201) and explored in detail by Mørch (2018) is the Integrated Information Theory (IIT), formulated originally by Giulio Tononi (2004) and developed further by Tononi in collaboration with various authors (e.g. Oizumi et al., 2014). Through a mathematical formula, Tononi and other proponents of IIT attempt to show how, when a sufficient level of information integration takes place in a complex system, the resulting integrated information is such that it can no longer be considered to be localized in any of the system's individual parts, instead becoming in a sense 'more than the sum of its parts'. The resulting sum of integrated information (labelled phi, Φ) is then taken to correlate with the 'degree' of consciousness in the system in question. A further criterion is then given: a system forms a unified subject if and only if it is a *maximum* of Φ, that is, if the system has a higher degree of information integration than any of its parts or any system of which it is itself a part (e.g. Mørch 2018, p. 3).

The information integration of IIT could therefore be a possible further criterion for phenomenal bonding. The end result of such a marriage would basically be the following: spatiotemporally and transitively connected microsubjects, which make up the intrinsic natures of microphysical ultimates, combine to form unified macrosubjects when their combination, taken as a complex system, has a degree of information integration higher than any of its parts or any system it is itself a part of. This would then work first to avoid the problem of the many, since it basically restricts the existence of subjects to only one subject per complex system, eliminating the possibility of various overlapping subjects; and secondly to avoid a cosmic subject, since it is entirely plausible that the cosmos as an entirety has a lesser degree of information integration than the human nervous system. In other words, it is entirely plausible to think that the human nervous system as a whole possesses a higher degree of information integration than either any of its parts taken alone, or any system of which it is itself a part of, such as the cosmos. (ibid. p. 3–4).

This is probably the most plausible candidate for a working phenomenal bonding solution as of yet, as well as one of the most promising candidates for an overall solution to the combination problem. However, it does come with its own problems. As Mørch argues, the basic principles of IIT as it has been described so far by Tononi and associates are incompatible with panpsychism. Though delving into the matter in much depth is outside the scope

CHAPTER FIVE

of the current work, suffice it to say that the tension lies in IIT being a functionalistic theory of consciousness, which allows for the multiple realizability of identical phenomenal states in systems which nevertheless have different dispositional properties. Since in panpsychism the phenomenal states are taken to be the quiddities of dispositional or structural properties, and are thus supposed to act as the 'carriers' of the dispositional properties, this lack of correlation between the two is problematic. (ibid., p. 10–12). However, it remains to be seen whether this tension is unsolvable or not. Mørch suggests that a modification of either the Exclusion principle of IIT—the principle that only the system with the highest degree of information integration is a unified subject—or its functionalistic nature could perhaps make it compatible with panpsychism (p. 14–18).

Let us again tally the score, then. Phenomenal bonding, like infusionism, has some wedge against the subject-summing problem, but as such only with the cost of some level of mysterianism. Bonding fares much better than infusionism against the structural mismatch problem, but Goff's initial solution of postulating bonding as the quiddity of spatiotemporal connectivity requires modification. Both the subject-summing problem and the structural mismatch problem could find a strong response in an alliance of IIT and phenomenal bonding—yet this alliance requires quite a bit of modification in turn to be made coherent. Though Strawson (2016) disagrees, the quality combination problem and the palette problem do seem to make up perhaps the most difficult of the three problems for phenomenal bonding, requiring *ad hoc* speculative work to function even at a conceptual level. Still, phenomenal bonding, especially in a mutually compatible alliance with IIT, remains one of the more promising candidates for a working panpsychistic framework.

5.2.2 Priority Cosmopsychism

I have described the core ideas of priority cosmopsychism already above in chapter 3.3, so I will go over them here only briefly. As explained in 3.3, the idea of priority cosmopsychism is to ground the macrophenomenal not in the microphenomenal, as in smallist versions of panpsychism, but instead in the cosmophenomenal—the phenomenality of the cosmos as a whole, taken as a single, all-subsuming subject. Shani (2015) expresses this basic postulate of cosmopsychism as the idea that "*the cosmos as a whole is the only ontological ultimate* there is, and... *it is conscious*" (p. 408, emphasis in original). In priority cosmopsychism, all sub-cosmic subjects are *grounded by subsumption* in the cosmic subject, instead of being *grounded by analysis* in their constituent microsubjects (Goff 2017a, p. 220–225). Despite this reversal of fundamentality, at least the standard form of cosmopsychism remains a form of constitutive panpsychism, since it still agrees that the cosmic subject is constituted of *non-fundamental* macro- and microphenomenal parts, which are simply grounded in the whole of which they are part.

Cosmopsychism does not, technically, face the combination problem at all—in cosmopsychist models, the microphenomenal does not combine to form the macrophenomenal in the same sense as in smallist models; rather, the microphenomenal is derived from the macrophenomenal. This means that the less fundamental macrophenomenal does not have to be in principle analyzable to the microphenomenal or the microphysical, which saves us the trouble of explaining how the latter gives rise to the former. However, it does have its own analogue of the problem which is in many substantial regards similar to the combination problem: the *decombination* problem (Goff 2017a, p. 228), also called the *derivation* problem (Nagasawa & Wager 2016, p. 121) and the *decomposition* problem (Shani 2015, p. 390). All of these terms

CHAPTER FIVE

point to the same problem of explaining how the obviously existent macrophenomenal is derived from the cosmophenomenal. Miller (2018) phrases this problem from the point of view of the unity of consciousness: since the consciousness of a particular subject is always unified, how can the cosmic subject have internal, disunified breaches to correspond to the external breaches and boundedness of its constituent macrosubjects (p. 144)? Cosmopsychism also inherits whatever problems may assail priority monism in general. However, it is necessary here to emphasize that cosmopsychism is indeed committed only to priority monism, which is the doctrine that there exists only one *fundamental* entity, and it therefore allows for the existence of multiple non-fundamental entities; it is not committed to the significantly stronger thesis of *existence monism*, which postulates that there exists only one entity, period[52]. Miller (2018, p. 139) expresses this as a difference between a *world-only* view (the existence monist position) and a *world-first* view (the priority monist position).

To evaluate the viability of cosmopsychism we have to see if the shift in the pole of fundamentality from the microlevel to the cosmic level is of any help in alleviating the combination problem. Nagasawa and Wager (2016) claim that, although the specifics of the derivation are unclear due to our lack of epistemic access to the nature of the cosmic subject, the decombination/ derivation/decomposition problem is in principle still less threatening than the combination problem (p. 121). They refer to the more general derivation problem concerning all varieties of priority monism—the problem of how the various heterogenous macroscopic objects, the concrete parts of the cosmos, are derived from the whole—and state that the derivation problem of priority cosmopsychism is essentially an analogous problem, and has

---

[52] For an example of an explication and defence of existence monism against priority monism, see Horgan & Potrč (2012).

recourse to the same solutions. They take three solutions presented by Schaffer (2010) concerning the more general derivation problem of priority monism: a solution by way of distributional properties; by way of regionalized properties; and by way of regionalized instantiation. (Nagasawa and Wager 2016, p. 122–123). The solution by way of distributional properties would attribute the cosmos with properties of a form such as "being so-and-so filled up with such-and-such objects", like "being polka-dotted"[53]. The solution by way of regionalized properties would likewise attribute the cosmos with properties like "being spiked in region A" or "being flat in region B". The third case, the solution by way of regionalized instantiation, would be to say that the cosmos has the non-regional properties of e.g. "spikiness" and "flatness", but that they are *instantiated* only regionally. Due to these possible avenues of answering the general derivation problem of priority monism, Nagasawa and Wager declare cosmopsychism tentatively more viable than smallist forms of panpsychism (p. 123–124). However, though any of these solutions might possibly work to explain the heterogeneity of an ontologically primary cosmos in general, the case of subject decomposition has several unique facets to it which make it problematic: questions of conceivability and lack of logical entailment, and the perspective objection in particular. Before we move on to a more specific consideration of the decomposition problem and its analogues of the sub-problems of the combination problem, let us continue with a more general review of the possible merits of the shift in the pole of fundamentality involved in cosmopsychism.

Though Philip Goff has, in his earlier writings (2009, 2016), explicitly defended a form of smallist panpsychism of the

---

[53] This particular example is from Goff 2017a, p. 224, where he defends a cosmopsychist framework by way of utilizing distributional properties much like Nagasawa and Wager.

phenomenal bonding type, Goff (2017a) essentially capitulates in the face of the subject-summing problem as it assails smallist panpsychism, claiming that the problem is unsolvable in a smallist framework (p. 217–219). The primary reason for this capitulation is Goff's conclusion that subjects are ultimately irreducible: the existence of one subject cannot be reduced to the existence of other subjects, no matter which relations hold between them. Since smallist panpsychism entails that macrosubjects are grounded by analysis in microsubjects, the kind of reductive analysis required for the theory to work would have to be deflationary, i.e. it would have to define the macrosubject without quantifying over the macrosubject itself in the definition (which would circular); and furthermore, the analysis would have to be accessible *a priori*, since, by way of the conceivability argument, it would have to be such that the negation of the analysis is inconceivable. Goff first excludes traditional functional analyses on grounds of the epistemic gap between the purely functional or structural and the phenomenal—in other words, on the grounds that it is impossible to define the intrinsic phenomenal using only extrinsic, structural terminology[54]. He then argues that the only other plausible candidate for a deflationary analysis is a definition based on the conjunction of the microphenomenal and some co-consciousness or phenomenal bonding relation, but discounts this alternative as well, concluding that no such analysis can be given which does not quantify over the particular subject being defined. (Goff

---

[54] This is essentially the argument from intrinsic natures against physicalism, as described above in chapter 2.5. Other panpsychists naturally disagree with Goff's analysis; it might be possible, for example, to provide a deflationary analysis of a subject that refers to the structure of the phenomenal itself, thus including reference to both functional elements as well as intrinsic elements. Gregg Rosenberg's (2004, 2016) Theory of Natural Individuals, considered below in 5.2.3, is an example of a theory based on such analysis.

2017a, p. 209–214). He then concludes that the grounding by analysis of subjects is impossible (p. 217).

This is then Goff's primary motivation for cosmopsychism: that it does not require the grounding by analysis of subjects. Macrosubjects and microsubjects are, instead, grounded by subsumption in the cosmic subject; and this, Goff argues, does not entail the reducibility of the less fundamental to the more fundamental. The idea here is that if the ontology of the cosmos is priority monist and the only fundamental entity, the cosmos itself, includes all other entities as non-fundamental parts or "aspects", to use Goff's preferred term, this already implies that the various aspects of the cosmos are nothing over and above the cosmos itself. In a cosmopsychist framework, we do not have to reduce the subjectivity of a macrosubject to its constituents or its structural features to achieve intelligible grounding; instead, we have recourse to a much simpler relation of inclusion, where the macrosubject is seen as nothing over and above the cosmic subject in virtue of literally being included in it[55]. Cosmopsychism would then avoid the problem of having to deliver a deflationary analysis of subjecthood, and would thus stand in a much better position to answer its decombination problem than smallist panpsychism its respective combination problem.

Shani (2015, p. 398–403) and Shani and Keppler (2018, p. 394) argue for cosmopsychism primarily by way of the perspective objection. As we have seen, the perspective objection pivots around the idea that the subjective experiences of singular subjects are by their nature such that they exclude other experiences; that they are essentially *points of view*, which by

---

[55] Whether or not this solution is actually so obvious and straightforward seems to me to be an open question; however, deeper probing of the matter will have to remain outside of this work, though deserving of further research and consideration.

CHAPTER FIVE

their very nature are unique, total, and bounded. Points of view cannot combine to form larger points of view. For such combination to be possible, the lower order points of view would have to literally exist as such as parts of the higher order point of view—but then they would lose their boundedness and their point-of-viewness. They would thus be unable to survive as bounded point of views of their own, while simultaneously being a part of a higher order point of view (Shani 2015, p. 401). One might argue that, though the points of view as such might not survive the combination, the *qualities* appearing to those points of view, those subjects, could survive and become parts of the experience of the higher order subject. However, this is not enough, since subject-summing would require the subjects themselves to sum and to survive the summing for the relation to be validly a compositional one[56] (ibid.). The conclusion then is that "perspectives do not combine, and hence neither do subjects" (ibid., p. 402).

Shani's idea is to a remarkable extent the same as Goff's, although utilizing different terminology. He takes the position that macrosubjects are only *partially grounded* in the cosmic subject; that though they are dependent on the cosmic subject, their nature is not "exhausted by this particular dependency relationship" (p. 422). For Shani, individual, sub-cosmic subjects share a *generic character* that is directly derived from the subjectivity of the cosmic consciousness, but that they each have a *specific character* as well, a "unique individual profile" which ensures their individual perspective (ibid.). The gist here is that their being subjects and sharing in subjectivity is their general

---

[56] One alternative to compositional subject-summing is naturally that of emergentism, where the survival of the constituents making up the emergence base is not necessary. Emergentism and its problems in general have been explored above in chapter 3.1, and infusionism as a specific type of emergentism in chapter 5.1.1.

character, whereas their being an individual point of view is their specific character—and only the general character is grounded in the cosmic consciousness (p. 423). The cosmic subject is then seen as "an intrinsically sentient universal medium" out of which individual subjects emerge as some kind of localized patterns of interference (p. 426), which Shani describes by way of analogy as localized *vortices* in the cosmic medium (p.419). The exact nature of these localized patterns is left quite unclear, however, as is the process of their arising.

Shani and Keppler (2018) build upon the framework presented in Shani (2015) with a fairly remarkable addition: a commitment to a particular theory of quantum mechanics, Stochastic Electrodynamics (SED), which emphasizes the importance of the *zero-point field* (ZPF), an all-pervasive electromagnetic field with random energy fluctuations (p. 396–399). The SED model is essentially an extension of the DeBroglie-Bohm interpretation of quantum mechanics[57], with the ZPF acting as the guiding pilot wave postulated in the larger framework of the DeBroglie-Bohm interpretation (Davidson 2006). SED postulates that the ZPF interacts continuously with all matter in a process of constant mutual influence: fluctuations in the ZPF cause changes in matter, and changes in matter partly condition fluctuations in the ZPF. Shani and Keppler present a fairly detailed overview of SED and how the ZPF and matter interact in the model, but suffice it here to say that, according to the authors, the interaction is such that coherent material structures essentially come into being as 'filtrations' of the zero-point energy field, and that finally "all physical properties of matter can be understood as... resulting from the interaction with the background field" (p. 398).

---

[57] For a detailed overview of DeBroglie-Bohm mechanics from the point of view of the philosophy of mind and consciousness, see Pylkkänen (2007).

CHAPTER FIVE

The authors' next move is highly reminiscent of Turausky's (unpublished) fundamental tone, as mentioned above in 5.2.1. They claim that the ZPF plays a dual role as the primordial source of all energy, as well as the fundamental carrier of consciousness, in which "all conceivable shades of phenomenal awareness are inherent" (p. 399)[58]. From the physical, empirical point of view the ZPF is seen as a vibrant field of activity, but from the intrinsic, phenomenal point of view it is seen as a "formless sea of consciousness" (ibid.). The idea then is that all phenomenal awareness, all subjectivity as a general property, is a filtration from the fundamental and all-encompassing tone or frequency of the ZPF, which includes, much like white light, the potentialities of all possible phenomenal experiences.

The authors' intention is that, in this model, neither the qualities nor the structure of the phenomenality of any subject is composed of or derived from the phenomenality of any other subject. The idea is, rather, that each individual subject gets its quality and structure from direct, resonant interaction with the ZPF. They come about as functions of the *relation* between the subject and the ZPF. Thus no subject is constituted of other subjects, and neither is any subject the part of another subject. To quote the authors at some length:

> "[I]nsofar as the present problem is concerned, the main point is that no subject is phenomenally composed of or fractured from another subject; rather, each subject obtains its phenomenal character by tapping directly into the universal pool of cosmic consciousness immanent to the ZPF and by extracting from it a system-specific set of correlated resonance frequencies". (p. 401).

---

[58] As far as I understand, the fundamental tone would essentially make up the implicate order of the Bohmian interpretation, in which all potentiality is implicit. The explicit material and phenomenal structure of reality would then be the actualized explicate order.

PANPSYCHISM AND THE COMBINATION PROBLEM

They go on to describe that though all the particular phenomenal nuances of all potential experiences do exist in a way in the fundamental tone of the ZPF, they do so in a dormant and undifferentiated manner—they exist only potentially, rather than actually (ibid.).

The mechanics of this filtration are thus far still unclear. Shani and Keppler attempt to sketch a model of these mechanics via reference to the underlying physics as well as Shani's (2015) analogy of a vortex in a background medium. SED, the physical background model for the theory, includes the idea that concrete physical objects, too, get their properties and form through a *resonance* with the ZPF. Quantum physical systems achieving a *resonant equilibrium* with the ZPF exist over time as patterns of locally organized intensity, which interact constantly with their surroundings, but are functionally demarcated from those surroundings. Shani and Keppler argue that this functional isolation is enough to produce at least a minimal separation of 'here', meaning the localized organization of intensity or the "vortex", and 'there', meaning the vortex's surroundings; this separation gives the localized vortices a kind of boundedness. The interactions of each vortex with its material surroundings are determined by its individual structure, itself a result of its individual interaction with the background ZPF; this limits the interactions of the vortex with its environment to "specific modes of opening to the world" (p. 404). All these characteristics in tandem—the vortices' relative stability as temporally enduring patterns of activity; their boundedness; and the limitation of their interactions to specific modes—could, according to the authors, be enough to establish the perspectival subjectivity and unity of a subject. (ibid.). The idea in a nutshell is then that quantum interaction with the ZPF is phenomenal activity, and that this phenomenal activity gets organized into more and more complex, relatively isolated subjects by way of self-reinforcing feedback

CHAPTER FIVE

loops with both the ZPF and the material surroundings of the subject. None of the subjects is constituted by any other subject, nor do they constitute any other subject. The ZPF is the primordial reservoir of subjectivity, the cosmic consciousness, in which all individual subject-vortices are born, and of which they all take part.

We have now considered the priority cosmopsychist answers to the decombination problem from several angles: that of Nagasawa and Wager (2016), who claim that answers dealing with object derivation in priority monism in general might suffice; that of Goff (2017a), who claims that the cosmopsychist is much better equipped to solve their decombination problem than the smallist their combination problem, since the former does not imply the reducibility of subjects; and that of Shani (2015) and Shani and Keppler (2018), who, like Goff, take subjects to be irreducible to each other, but who further develop the idea by conjoining it with a plausible physical mechanism of non-constitutive subject generation. I believe that the problems of subject derivation and perspectival combination and decombination are such that they make up a special case of derivation that is essentially distinct from object derivation in general. Even though appeals to distributional properties and the likes may serve as sketches of how heterogeneity in the material world could appear in a priority monist framework, the generation of separate subjects is a much more sophisticated problem. I therefore do not think that Nagasawa's and Wager's suggestion for this kind of more general, simple solution is tenable. The solutions of Goff on one hand and Shani & Shani and Keppler on the other are both based on the idea that subjects are irreducible (and thus irreducible *a fortiori* to the distributional properties of the cosmos); but out of these two solutions that of Shani and Keppler seems to me more sophisticated. I shall thereby concentrate in the following on their model.

PANPSYCHISM AND THE COMBINATION PROBLEM

How does cosmopsychism as it is presented here deal, then with the decombination problem and its sub-problems? The most promising answer to the subject-derivation problem thus far presented is that of Shani and Keppler: that subjects do not, in fact, sum; and thus neither are they derived from each other. Their phenomenal character is a unique generation from their interaction with the cosmic consciousness, but only weakly emergent, if the background physics of the model check out. Other models of subject-derivation may of course be presented, but as of yet, all the other suggestions are fairly tentative. However, as the authors themselves admit (p. 405), it still might be argued that the existence of a background field of energy and all its fluctuations (as considered from the physical perspective) do not logically entail the existence of phenomenality. In other words, the conjunction of the physical model and the negation of all phenomenal facts might still remain conceivable. But *if* the background physics of the model checks out and *if* we accept the speculative assumption that the background ZPF is the primordial reservoir of consciousness, the physical model might, under careful consideration and perhaps after some further explication and clarification of the suggested mechanisms of phenomenal differentiation, be seen to entail the existence of the kind of macrosubjects that we humans appear to be. The primary vulnerability of Shani and Keppler's model is, then, its commitment to a particular quantum mechanical theory, which has not yet achieved widespread acceptance in its own field. As comes to the quality combination problem, the answer is for the most part the same: the qualities of separate subjects do not combine, since subjects themselves do not combine. The palette problem is avoided because, instead of macrophenomenal qualities being constituted of microphenomenal qualities, the phenomenal qualities on all levels of nature arise from the interaction and resonance of the particular subject with the

CHAPTER FIVE

background field of cosmic consciousness. The cosmic consciousness is essentially a Turausky fundamental tone: an undifferentiated frequency of phenomenality which, much like white light includes in itself the potentiality of all the colors, includes the potentiality of all possible phenomenal experiences. The qualities of particular subjects are filtrations of this all-encompassing fundamental frequency, which take the form they have in particular subjects due to their individual, specific material structure and the interaction of this structure with the ZPF of cosmic consciousness. The perspective objection does not arise, since subjects are not included as constituents in each other.

In terms of the structural mismatch problem, the viability of the Shani/Keppler model depends, again, 1) on its conformity and compatibility with its background physics and 2) the viability of the background physics as physical theory. If both of these check out, the authors have recourse to the hypothesis that the structure of the macrophenomenal is isomorphic to the structure of quantum fluctuations in the nervous system, the resonance of the physical structure with the background ZPF. This would then dissolve the structural mismatch problem, because the theory would then include a physics that corresponds to the theory's model of phenomenal structure and generation.

To tally the score: Priority cosmopsychism, as described and developed by Shani and Keppler, manages to answer all the sub-problems of the decombination problem with fairly high success, although the mechanisms of subject derivation could use some further explication and clarification. The only major problem is that the theory rests so essentially on its background physics—and seeing that the physics are, as physical theory, contested and without widespread acceptance, the viability of cosmopsychism is still left in the air. It is of course not totally out of the question that alternative accounts of cosmopsychism without such commitments could perhaps be developed in the future.

5.2.3 The Theory of Natural Individuals

Gregg Rosenberg's (2004, 2016) Theory of Natural Individuals (TNI) is the odd one out in this taxonomy of hypotheses. In comparison with the other theories, which still work within a somewhat traditional general metaphysical framework, TNI comes with a lot of additional metaphysical baggage—a commitment to a particular theory of causation as well as an entirely novel ontology.

Since Rosenberg's views on consciousness rest crucially on his theory of causation, I shall begin my exposition there. Rosenberg argues that, to make better sense of the world, we should move away from theories of causal *responsibility* to theories of causal *significance* (2004, p. 150–152). Rosenberg views the basic units of causality not as traditional and temporally asymmetric cause and effect relations, where first one event takes place and in taking place mechanically causes another later event to take place, but as mutually conditioning and excluding *potentiality filters*. Rosenberg sees the world as a vast system of events which, according to the empirical, fixed natural laws of physics either exclude or allow other potential events. He presents a metaphor of a magical canvas which allows only particular combinations of colors to stick to it. Depending on the colors already on the canvas, it accepts only certain additions in any particular place—and the more paint there is on the canvas, the pickier it becomes. (2016, p. 158–159). "Every color and every drop matters, jointly enforcing or excluding the colors that will finally appear on the canvas" (p. 159). The point is that no singular drop of color on the canvas causes any other drop to appear, but that each drop is an essentially significant part of the entire system of colors, which as a whole reduces, according to natural law, the probability space for the manifestation of any new droplets of color until only one non-contradictory possibility remains. This possibility is then manifested as an actual,

CHAPTER FIVE

determinate droplet of color on the canvas. Thus, there is no monolithic causal responsibility—only causal significance. This process has nothing inherently temporal about it, and neither is it temporally asymmetric. Neither is there any hierarchy of levels. Theoretically, future events could restrict past potentialities, and events of a higher level of nature could restrict events of a lower level of nature (ibid.).

Rosenberg argues for his view of causality on the basis of a correspondence with how causality is handled in the natural sciences. In particular, he points to the seeming indeterminacy of the microphysical level in quantum physics, where it seems both that properties at the microphysical level can be dependent on events at the macrolevel, such as observation; and also that events happening at a great distance from each other can affect each other, as in quantum entanglement. Neither top-down causation or causation at a distance is inherently a problem for a theory of causal significance, since causation is deflated of any causally responsible 'contact', and is seen instead only as a system of mutually conditioning and excluding potentiality filters.

With this general sketch of Rosenberg's theory of causation in hand we can now move on to describe his ontology. The ontology consists of two types of fundamental properties, one fundamental relation, and natural laws. The two types of properties are *effective properties*, which bind to each other and inherently contribute to probability constraints in a particular *causal nexus*, which essentially means a single individual thing, like an electron; and *receptive properties*, which essentially form the background or space in which effective properties can bind to each other, which creates a causal nexus (2016, p. 162–163). For Rosenberg, an individual thing like an electron is essentially a bundle of mutually conditioning effective properties, like mass, spin and charge, and a receptive property through which the effective properties can bind together, forming a causal nexus.

PANPSYCHISM AND THE COMBINATION PROBLEM

Rosenberg further explicates that isolated effective properties, separated from any causal nexus in which they are bound to other effective properties, remain in ontologically indeterminate states—when so isolated, they are to some extent like uninstantiated universals. Unless the spin of an electron, for example, is really bound to the other properties of an electron such as mass and charge, within the space of a single receptive property, it does not have any specific, determined state or value. (p. 163). "Properties *need* context (causal binding to other things) to be anything in particular" (ibid., original emphasis). The binding together of effective properties in a causal nexus adds more and more constraints to the values or states of the properties in a process of mutual conditioning according to the laws of nature. The binding together of properties thus makes them progressively more and more determinate, each constraint reducing the probability space for the states of all the participant properties in the nexus. No single property in the nexus *causes,* in a monolithic sense, the value of any other property—but they are all *causally significant* in the sense of constraining the probability spaces for those values. This is causation within a particular causal nexus, which happens within one level of nature. However, this kind of causation is not enough to fully determine (i.e. to fully reduce the probability spaces of) the properties involved in the nexus, much like the spin of an electron, for example, seems from the physical perspective to have no determinate value if the electron is considered as an isolated particle. The initial causal nexus, such as the isolated electron, can itself act as an effective, constraining property in a causal nexus of a higher order, with a similar structure of effective properties and a receptive property. In this higher order nexus, the other effective properties then exert further constraints on the electron, the lower order nexus. This structure of nested, recursive hierarchy then repeats on yet higher and higher levels of nature, which exert further and further constraints on all the lower order nexii, until finally the probability

CHAPTER FIVE

space of the spin of the initial electron is reduced to only one possible value, with the spin finally being actualized in a determinate state. There is once again a reference here to quantum physics and the Heisenbergian indeterminacy of quantum level properties, which, according to the standard interpretation of quantum mechanics, require the intervention of an observer to become determinate; the observation is a process of binding of the observed electron into a hierarchy of causal nexii, which ultimately constrains the properties of the electron in such a way that they are forced to assume determinate values. This would then be an example of top-down causation, causation from a higher level of nature to a lower level. In Rosenberg's theory, then, this process of binding and mutual constraining within and across different levels of nature is what causal interactions are. (2016, p. 163–165).

We have now gone over the concept of causation as well as the ontology of Rosenberg's theory, and have the necessary equipment to consider his views on consciousness and phenomenal combination. Rosenberg first argues alongside Armstrong (1997), Russell (1927) and others, that causal properties *qua* causal are extrinsic in nature, and require an intrinsic base to act as a "carrier" for the functional, structural and dispositional extrinsic properties (Rosenberg 2016, p. 166). The intrinsic properties acting as this base would have to be isomorphic to the purely extrinsic, causal description given above, showing the same structure of causal nexii with effective and receptive properties. Consciousness, Rosenberg concludes, has exactly the kind of properties required of such an intrinsic nature: it is, in itself, a contentless field of receptivity in which appear mutually conditioning, allowing and excluding[59]

---

[59] For example, the phenomenal properties of something filling a large portion of the visual field and that thing being red are mutually allowing properties; whereas the same object being green and red are mutually excluding properties.

phenomenal properties. The idea, then, is that consciousness is the continuous process of *shared receptivity* between effective properties seeking determinacy in a causal nexus. Any causal nexus, made up of a receptive property and two or more bound effective properties, forms, in a sense a subject. The isomorphism of consciousness to the causal structure would then, in other words, be as follows: a unified subject is a single, bound causal nexus made up of a receptive property—the contentless field of awareness—bound up with numerous effective properties—the qualia, or phenomenal properties. (Rosenberg 2016, p. 167).

Next, the combination problem. Rosenberg's theory gives out a model of the structure of conscious subjects and their place in the world—it not only postulates that the intrinsic natures of empirically observable entities are phenomenal, but also explains *why* they are phenomenal: they are phenomenal because 1) the causal structure of reality requires intrinsic properties as carriers; 2) the intrinsic properties must form a structure isomorphic to the causal structure of reality; and 3) phenomenality and subjectivity are structurally isomorphic to the causal structure. To quote Rosenberg:

> "[S]omeone trying to make sense of [causal significance] in the world will feel compelled to hypothesize that phenomenal properties are the intrinsic basis of effective properties; and that an experiential property is the intrinsic basis of receptive connection; and that the causal nexus in our world is carried by the experiencing of phenomenal properties by the carrier of the receptive connection. The experiencing of phenomenal properties is the causal nexus in our world. Anywhere there is direct interaction between natural individuals, there we will find the occurrence of experiencing." (2016, p. 167; emphasis in original).

CHAPTER FIVE

Rosenberg refers to *natural individuals* in the quote above, which is his term for unified subjects. The question of what constitutes a natural individual is then, for Rosenberg, the crux of the combination problem.

In TNI, there are two types of natural individuals, both of which constitute unified subjects:

> "Base rule: Any primitive receptive or primitive effective property is a natural individual[60]. Recursive combination rule: Any receptive property, which completes itself by binding to two or more other natural individuals is a natural individual." (2016, p. 165)

Any unbound receptive or effective property constitutes a natural individual. All *completed* causal nexii are also natural individuals. A causal nexus, again, is the conjunction of a receptive property and at least two primitive effective properties or other natural individuals bound with that receptive property. A causal nexus (or receptive connection) is completed only if it serves to reduce the probability space of at least one of its constituent effective properties; that is to say, only if it makes the state of at least one of its constituent effective properties more determinate.

> "A completed receptive connection has (1) at least one constituent with an indeterminate state when considered independently of its membership in the nexus, and (2) a common receptivity being shared by two or more constituents. The shared receptivity establishes a

---

[60] Rosenberg refers to Keith Turausky's (unpublished) idea of the fundamental tone, speculating that the phenomenality of primitive properties could be all-encompassing and unfiltered, much in the same way that white light encompasses all the colors. Turausky's suggestion is considered further below due to its prominence in Rosenberg's answer to the quality combination problem.

connection between the members of the nexus through which they contribute to a set of simultaneous constraints on their joint states." (Rosenberg 2004, p. 286).

Only causal nexii that serve as completed receptive connections are natural individuals; thus, only they are unified, experiencing subjects. This is because, for Rosenberg, the process of living, changing experience is *exactly* the process of causality, meaning the mutual conditioning between effective properties, the process of progressive mutual determination of otherwise indeterminate properties and individuals. This means that for there to be phenomenality and experience there has to be causal interaction, in other words, mutual determination. For there to be mutual determination in a causal nexus, the nexus has to include at least one effective property which is to some degree determined in virtue of participating as part of the nexus. And for an effective property to be determined in virtue of participating as part of the nexus, its state must be at least to some degree indeterminate when considered in isolation from the nexus. This is why the nexus has to include at least one effective property the state of which is indeterminate when considered in isolation from the nexus; once again, the causal nexus has to make the state of at least one bound effective property more determinate.

This gives us a general answer to the subject-summing problem: subjects are natural individuals, which sum when their summing makes their states more determinate, through the mechanism of binding to a receptive property and entering into a mutually conditioning and determining connection. Properties are drawn to determinacy (completion) much like atoms are drawn to an octet state. Higher-level subjects exist because they are necessary to determine the states of lower-level subjects.

Rosenberg (2016) explicitly suggests that this model is both compatible and much reinforced by other more empirically

CHAPTER FIVE

minded theories of consciousness. He promotes a synthesis of TNI with the Integrated Information Theory of Tononi (e.g. 2004), the Global Workspace Theory of Bernard Baars (e.g. 2002), and the Dynamic Core and Thalamo-Cortical Resonance Theory of Edelman and Tononi (e.g. 2000), with the idea that each of these theories describes respectively higher and higher orders of reality (p. 169). Since TNI alone describes only the general mechanisms of subjectivity and subject-summing, it does not yet give much indication as to which objects actually fulfil the criteria for subjectivity. Rosenberg's idea is that Tononi's IIT, with its empirically quantifiable Φ, could work as a system of indicating the presence of conscious natural individuals (p. 171). Likewise, the Global Workspace Theory of Baars could name criteria to distinguish between systems involving only phenomenal consciousness or experientiality, and those involving access consciousness[61] and cognition, while Dynamic Core theories can shed light on how exactly consciousness is instantiated in the mammalian brain (p. 171–172). Taken together these theories form what Rosenberg calls the *synoptic pyramid* of consciousness, building up to a more or less complete theory of consciousness (p. 168).

In terms of the subject-summing problem, Rosenberg's suggested solution is certainly very elegant and powerful. If both its background ontology and theory of causation, as well as Rosenberg's vision of a synoptic alliance with the other theories of consciousness[62], are accepted, it certainly seems to give a strong answer to the problem. The theory's biggest weaknesses

---

[61] The difference between phenomenal consciousness and access consciousness is explained already in chapter 1.3.

[62] As considered in chapter 5.2.1, Integrated Information Theory might not be compatible with at least the usual varieties of panpsychism. I am not as of yet certain whether this deeper incompatibility holds also between IIT and Rosenberg's idiosyncratic theory. This question has to be left for further research.

are indeed exactly these significant background commitments. A proper, in-depth evaluation of TNI's ontology and theory of causation would seem to me to require much more work than can be allocated to it in the current work; suffice it to say that though criticism can likely be raised against the theory, at least *prima facie* its correspondence with how causation is dealt with in the natural sciences, as well as its explanatory power as comes to some empirical physical observations of quantum phenomena, can be taken as significant merits. As Rosenberg writes, though his theory of causal significance may be exotic in the metaphysical literature, all it actually is is a metaphysical reconstruction of the standard model of quantum mechanics (2016, p. 164).

Next, the quality combination problem. In the TNI framework, phenomenal qualities are seen as the intrinsic natures of causal effective properties. These effective properties constitute natural individuals (subjects) in tandem with receptive properties. These individuals then act as effective properties in higher order causal nexii, constituting higher order natural individuals. In this architecture, the higher order subjects quite literally consist of the lower order subjects bound within the field of a new receptive property, meaning that the qualitative landscape of higher order individuals should also incorporate the qualities of lower order individuals, unless an alternative structure of quality combination is presented.

Rosenberg refers to Turausky's (unpublished) idea of the fundamental tone, arguing that qualities do not actually combine from simple, primitive qualities to form more complex qualities, but are instead filtered out from a ubiquitous fundamental quale (2016, p. 173). This would essentially solve the quality combination problem, since instead of qualities combining to form higher order macroqualities, the lower order microqualities are instead 'stripped' of elements until what is left is the final

CHAPTER FIVE

macroquality. When we considered Turausky's idea as part of our discussion of phenomenal bonding theories and the quality combination problem in chapter 5.2.1, we remarked that it remained quite *ad hoc* and did not have much independent motivation. However, in terms of Rosenberg's theory the idea has much more motivation due to a very high congruence with the theory's background ontology and the theory of causal significance. Recall that in Rosenberg's theory the very phenomenon of experientiality and subjectivity is essentially the causal process of determination, where primitive properties which are highly indeterminate when isolated from other properties become more and more determinate when bound together in a phenomenal causal nexus. The combination of the natural individuals thus formed is in its essential function a process of further and further determination. The idea that macroqualities are filtrations of a ubiquitous, fundamental tone is highly congruent with the view of subject-summing as a reduction of indeterminacy in the space of possible states of primitive properties, progressing from complete indeterminacy towards a state of complete determinacy. In both cases the elementary state is a state of absolute potentiality, which is then reduced in the process of combination and structural sophistication. The combination of TNI and the fundamental tone thus seems to perform excellently as comes to quality combination and the palette problem.

Let us then consider the perspective objection. The qualitative states of higher order individuals are literally constituted from lower order individuals, which act as effective properties (phenomenal qualities) in the higher order causal nexii. If we believe the background assumptions of the perspective objection and accept that some qualitative properties can essentially be such that they exclude other properties, it is unclear how these mutually exclusive properties could constitute the phenomenality

PANPSYCHISM AND THE COMBINATION PROBLEM

of a higher order subject. However, this ought not to form a significant challenge for TNI due to its ontology of less and more determinate properties and how it already includes mutually exclusive properties in its basic framework. In TNI, it is already impossible in virtue of the model itself for mutually exclusive *determinate* properties to exist in the same causal nexus or hierarchy of nexii. Lower order qualities are indeterminate in nature, with a wide range of potential states they could be in; their nature is essentially disjunctive. All the disjuncts mutually exclude each other, so that if one state becomes determinate, it excludes all the others; but the disjuncts also effect constraints on other properties in the same causal nexus. When the lower order individual/nexus is joined into a higher order nexus, the other individuals in that higher order nexus effect additional constraints on all the properties of the initial lower order nexus. In a nutshell, only some of the disjuncts of the possibility space of an indeterminate lower level property exclude some possible states of any other particular property, with some of the disjuncts of the first individual lower level property also allowing other states of the second property. The final configuration of the entire hierarchy of lower and higher order individuals in which the lower order property takes part determines which states all the properties in the hierarchy take, so that the end result is one of mutual compatibility between all the properties. Once again, due to the ontology of TNI, it is impossible for mutually exclusive determinate properties to exist as part of the same nexus or hierarchy of nexii. TNI thus seems to avoid the perspective objection entirely.

Finally, the structural mismatch problem. This one has the simplest answer. As explained above, Rosenberg's theory of causation postulates a causal structure which is isomorphic to the structure of phenomenality and subjectivity. If the theory of causal significance holds, the structural mismatch problem is

CHAPTER FIVE

dissolved—the structural congruence, though perhaps not found between the empirically observed brain as a macrophysical structure and the phenomenal structure of human macroexperience, is actually found already on the much more fundamental level of causation itself. Since the Theory of Natural Individuals in its entirety rests essentially on the theory of causal significance, it is not very meaningful to question the latter as a separate assumption. TNI rises and falls with the theory of causal significance, and if it holds, it can easily solve the structural mismatch problem.

Let us once again tally the score. If the background assumptions and ontology of TNI are accepted, the theory seems to have great promise in solving all of the three sub-problems of the combination problem. It presents a model of both the structure and mechanism of subject-summing; manages to give a tentative answer to the quality combination and palette problems via Turausky's idea of the fundamental tone, with much higher congruence than a similar answer in connection with phenomenal bonding theories; it avoids the perspective objection in virtue of its ontology of variant determinacy; and presents an ontology isomorphic to the structure of phenomenality, dissolving the structural mismatch problem. Furthermore, TNI manages to give, through its ontology, an explanation for why phenomenality and subjectivity are what they are, which other theories have not been able to do. In summary, if the background metaphysics of TNI checks out, and especially if its postulated alliances with the other more empirically minded contemporary theories of consciousness can be brought to fruition, the theory stands as certainly one of the most promising candidates for an answer to the combination problem.

CHAPTER SIX
CONCLUSIONS AND DISCUSSION

It is now time to bring this work to a close. In the course of this book, we have first taken as our axiom that phenomenal consciousness exists—that phenomenal concepts have referents. We then considered physicalism, especially emergent physicalism, and its capabilities in answering the hard problem of consciousness and closing the explanatory gap between the phenomenally sterile, purely physical on the one hand and the phenomenal on the other. We concluded that emergent physicalism faces several deep problems in this project: first, it has significant difficulty in explaining the emergence of the phenomenal in any intelligible way, and has to resort to brute/radical/superstrong emergence; second, it cannot by virtue of the limitations of physical and all empirical science name any reasonable candidates for what any intrinsic properties might be like; and third, it is critically endangered by the conceivability argument (which, it must be said, does rest on the still debated jump from conceivability to metaphysical possibility). These three problems served as our principal motivation for exploring panpsychism as an alternative which could avoid all three. After delineating the varieties of panpsychism using the three axes of constitutivism/non-constitutivism, panpsychism/panprotopsychism, and smallism/priority cosmopsychism, the combination problem and its three sub-problems of subject-summing, quality combination and

CHAPTER SIX

structural mismatch were presented. Following this came the longest part of them all, a description and analysis of four contemporary approaches to the combination problem, along with their respective frameworks.

There are some conclusions I would like to reiterate here. First of all, I believe the problems facing physicalism are so severe that it is high time for us to move past the traditional physicalist framework towards a more neutral monist framework. Due to the argument from intrinsic natures, I believe some form of panpsychism to be by far the best alternative currently available. However, a related conclusion I would like here to make is that the motivation for panpsychism is indeed quite dependent on the necessity of intrinsic properties: if intrinsic properties are somehow done away with entirely, as in some ontic structural realist theories (see e.g. Ladyman et al. 2007), our most important reason for turning to panpsychism in particular falls as well. In the current work the highly important question of whether intrinsic properties are in fact necessary or not has not been given all that much space and depth of analysis. This is one field of study which I feel is of high importance in laying a proper, solid foundation for the panpsychist project. I do believe that if we take the Consciousness Constraint seriously, and believe that there are such things as phenomenal properties to which phenomenal terms refer, these properties cannot be seen as anything other than intrinsic properties—in which case considerations of parsimony would be in favor of panpsychism as a view that unifies or makes continuous the range of intrinsic properties. The various carrier theses and related suggestions mentioned here and there in this work also point towards the necessity of intrinsic, categorical properties as the carriers of dispositional and structural properties. But this is still an open question.

Another conclusion I would like to make is that though there is still a lot of work to be done, at least two of the panpsychist

PANPSYCHISM AND THE COMBINATION PROBLEM

theories considered here, the Theory of Natural Individuals of Rosenberg, and the Priority Cosmopsychism of Shani and Keppler, are, in my mind, quite sophisticated and promising in answering our fundamental questions about consciousness. Rosenberg's theory has the additional significant theoretical merit of being able to give at least a tentative answer to why phenomenality is as it is; why it has the nature and structure it has. It is interesting, though, that both theories have something of a commitment to a particular interpretation of quantum mechanics—Shani's and Keppler's to Stochastic Electrodynamics and the DeBroglie-Bohm hidden variable interpretation, Rosenberg's to the standard Copenhagen interpretation—and at least currently these interpretations are mutually exclusive. However, Rosenberg's commitment is significantly lighter, since, whereas Shani and Keppler rely essentially on their particular physical theory of choice to explain the very mechanisms of their framework, in Rosenberg's case the foundation is more metaphysical, and the structural similarities to the Copenhagen interpretation more of a motivation than a dependency. I find myself curious about what a synthesis of these two theories—Rosenberg's TNI and priority cosmopsychism—would look like, and whether it would be possible; again one avenue for possible further research.

One interesting point of convergence between suggestions within the phenomenal bonding theories, Shani's and Keppler's priority cosmopsychism, and Rosenberg's theory, is that each of them utilizes to some extent the idea that fundamental phenomenality—be it the phenomenality of elementary particles or properties in smallism, or the background cosmic consciousness for Shani and Keppler—is all-inclusive and analogous to white light: the undifferentiated fundamental tone from which all other phenomenal qualities are filtered. This reversal from seeing the fundamental qualities as simple and

CHAPTER SIX

requiring complex combination to form the richness of macrophenomenal qualities, to seeing the fundamental as all-inclusive and requiring filtration to derive the definite and differentiated macrophenomenal, is currently the most promising solution to the palette problem, and since it is quite generally applicable, it is no wonder that it has gained so much prominence. However, though the idea is generally applicable, the strength of the motivation and congruence of the idea with the theory in question varies. Whereas the phenomenal bonding theorist has not much other motivation for adopting the fundamental tone than the *ad hoc* reason of solving the palette problem, the fundamental tone has much resonance and congruence with both the Shani/Keppler model as well as Rosenberg's theory: the former already postulates as a necessary part of the theory an undifferentiated background field of all-inclusive consciousness, whereas the latter sees elementary phenomenality as a yet indeterminate disjunction of all possible qualitative states that requires bonding to other properties to achieve any determinacy. In a sense, both theories already include the fundamental tone in their basic ontology.

It is interesting to consider the relationship of panpsychism to some forms of objective idealism, since these two general theories obviously have something in common. In a sense, panpsychism postulates that the intrinsic nature, what things are in themselves, is phenomenal, so mental, in a sense; and that this mentality exists objectively in all things, regardless of our perception. This is not all that far away from objective idealism. Leibnizian monadology, for example, might be surprisingly compatible with some forms of contemporary panpsychism, at the very least identity panpsychism, described in chapter 3.2. Chalmers (2020) explores the relationship between panpsychism and idealism in some detail, arguing for a fairly natural progression from materialism first to dualism, then to panpsychism and finally towards idealism. I believe there are good reasons to think that in a truly monist framework that incorporates both the phenomenal and the physical as manifestations of the same substance, the differences between objective idealism and materialism as they have traditionally been thought of fade away. With the advent of this kind of more truly monist framework we might finally drop the dialectic of mental versus physical, and the whole substance question along with it, as Rosenberg (2016, p. 155) suggests. Of course, questions about the relevance of perception to material formation—the impact of an observing subject on reality—remain intriguing and essential, as they do also in contemporary physics. The relevance of a Whiteheadian process or event ontology to the panpsychist project has been of high interest to me throughout this project, and although considerations of this alliance have not made it to this final version of the work, I encourage further research into this matter, and hope to investigate it myself in later work. Rosenberg's ontology, at the very least, is explicitly a process (or event) ontology (2016, p. 164), though the importance of this commitment is still unclear to me.

As a final remark, I would like to say that these are indeed very exciting times for the philosophy of consciousness and consciousness research. Novel suggestions incorporating both physical mechanism and philosophical work such as the Shani/Keppler model and Rosenberg's theory truly do seem to me to tentatively point to an upcoming synoptic, complete theory of consciousness. The congruence of these philosophical models with physics as well as more empirically minded theories of consciousness gives great promise for further research in the field of theoretical unification.

BIBILIOGRAPHY

Albahari, M. (2020). Beyond Cosmopsychism and the Great I Am: How the World Might Be Grounded in Universal 'Advaitic' Consciousness. In *The Routledge Handbook of Panpsychism,* W. Seager (ed.). Routledge.

Alter, T. & Nagasawa, Y. (2012). What is Russellian Monism?. *Journal of Consciousness Studies*, 19 (9–10): 67–95.

Armstrong, D. M. (1997). *A World of States of Affairs.* Cambridge University Press.

Baars, B. J. (2002). The Conscious Access Hypothesis: Origins and Recent Evidence. *Trends in Cognitive Sciences*, 6 (1): 47–52.

Bliss, R. & Trogdon, K. (2016). Metaphysical Grounding. *In The Stanford Encyclopedia of Philosophy (Winter 2016 edition)*, E. N. Zalta (ed.). https://plato.stanford.edu/entries/grounding/

Block, N. (1995). On a Confusion About a Function of Consciousness. *Behavioral and Brain Sciences*, 18(2): 227–247.

Bourget, D. & Chalmers, D. J. (2014). What Do Philosophers Believe? *Philosophical Studies*, 170 (3): 465–500. Available online at https://philpapers.org/archive/BOUWDP.

Broad, C. D. (1925). *Mind and Its Place in Nature.* Routledge and Kegan Paul.

Brüntrup, G. (2016). Emergent Panpsychism. In *Panpsychism,* G. Brüntrup & L. Jaskolla (eds.). Oxford University Press.

Brüntrup, G. & Jaskolla, L. (2016, eds.). *Panpsychism*. Oxford University Press.

Callicott, J. D. (1982). Traditional American Indian and Western European attitudes toward nature: An Overview. *Environmental Ethics*, 4: 293 –318.

Cerullo, M. A. (2015). The Problem with Phi: A Critique of Integrated Information Theory. *PLoS Comput Biol* 11(9). https://doi.org/10.1371/journal.pcbi.1004286.

Chalmers, D. J. (1995). Facing Up to the Problem of Consciousness. *Journal of Consciousness Studies*, 2(3): 200–219. Freely accessible at http://consc.net/papers/facing.html.

Chalmers, D. J. (1996). The Conscious Mind: In Search of a Fundamental Theory. Oxford University Press.

Chalmers, D. J. (2006): Strong and Weak Emergence. In *The Re-Emergence of Emergence*, P. Clayton & P. Davies (eds.). Oxford University Press.

Chalmers, D. J. (2009). The Two-Dimensional Argument Against Materialism. In *Oxford Handbook of the Philosophy of Mind*, B. P. McLaughlin (ed.). Oxford University Press.

Chalmers, D. J. (2016a). Panpsychism and Panprotopsychism. In *Panpsychism*, G. Brüntrup & L. Jaskolla (eds.). Oxford University Press.

Chalmers, D. J. (2016b): The Combination Problem for Panpsychism In *Panpsychism*, G. Brüntrup & L. Jaskolla (eds.). Oxford University Press.

Chalmers, D. J. (2020). Idealism and the Mind-Body Problem. In *The Routledge Handbook of Panpsychism,* W. Seager (ed.). Routledge.

Churchland, P. S. (2013). *Touching a Nerve*. W. W. Norton and Company.

BIBLIOGRAPHY

Coleman, S. (2006). Being Realistic: Why Physicalism May Entail Panexperientialism. *Journal of Consciousness Studies,* 13(10–11): 40–52.

Coleman, S. (2014). The Real Combination Problem: Panpsychism, Micro-subjects and Emergence. *Erkenntnis,* 79: 19–44.

Coleman, S. (2015). Neuro-Cosmology. In *Phenomenal Qualities: Sense, Perception and Consciousness,* P. Coates & S. Coleman (eds.). Oxford University Press.

Coleman, S. (2016). Panpsychism and Neutral Monism: How to Make Up One's Mind. In *Panpsychism,* G. Brüntrup & L. Jaskolla (eds.). Oxford University Press.

Dainton, B. (2000). Stream of Consciousness: Unity and Continuity in Conscious Experience. Routledge.

Davidson, M. P. (2006). Stochastic Models of Quantum Mechanics—A Perspective. In *Foundations of Probability and Physics–4,* G. Adenier, C. Fuchs & A. Khrennikov (eds.). American Institute of Physics.

Dennett, D. C. (1990). Quining Qualia. In *Mind and Cognition,* W. G. Lycan (ed.). MIT Press.

Edelman, G. M. & Tononi, G. (2000). *A Universe of Consciousness.* Basic Books.

Enqvist, K. (1998). Olemisen porteilla. WSOY.

Feigl, H. (1960). Mind-Body, Not a Pseudo-Problem. In *Dimensions of Mind,* S. Hook (ed.). New York University Press.

Fine, K. (2012). Guide to Ground. In *Metaphysical Grounding: Understanding the Structure of Reality,* F. Correia & B. Schnieder (eds.). Cambridge University Press.

Fisher, S. (2014). Pierre Gassendi. In *The Stanford Encyclopedia of Philosophy (Spring 2014 Edition),* E. N. Zalta (ed.). https://plato.stanford.edu/archives/spr2014/entries/gassendi/.

Flanagan, O. (1991). *Science of the Mind.* MIT Press.

Gazzaniga, M. S. (2005). Forty-five years of split-brain research and still going strong. *Nature Reviews Neuroscience*, 6(8): 653–659.

Goff, P. (2006). Experiences Don't Sum. *Journal of Consciousness Studies*, 13(6): 53–61.

Goff, P. (2009). Why Panpsychism Doesn't Help Us Explain Consciousness. *Dialectica*, 63(3): 289–311.

Goff, P. (2016). The Phenomenal Bonding Solution to the Combination Problem. In *Panpsychism*, G. Brüntrup & L. Jaskolla (eds.). Oxford University Press.

Goff, P. (2017a). *Consciousness and Fundamental Reality*. Oxford University Press.

Goff, P. (2017b). Panpsychism is crazy, but it's also most probably true. *Aeon Magazine*. Published online at https://aeon.co/ideas/panpsychism-is-crazy-but-its-also-most-probably-true.

Goff, P., Seager, W. & Allen-Hermanson, S. (2017). Panpsychism. *In The Stanford Encyclopedia of Philosophy (Winter 2017 edition)*, E. N. Zalta (ed.). https://plato.stanford.edu/archives/win2017/entries/panpsychism.

Horgan, T. & Potrč, M. (2012). Existence Monism Trumps Priority Monism. In *Spinoza on Monism*, P. Goff (ed.). Palgrave-Macmillan.

Jackson, F. (1982). Epiphenomenal Qualia. *Philosophical Quarterly*, 32(127): 127–136.

Jackson, F. (2006). Galen Strawson on Panpsychism. *Journal of Consciousness Studies*, 13(10–11): 62–64.

James, W. (1890/1950). *The Principles of Psychology*. Dover Publications.

James, W. (1896). *Is Life Worth Living?* S. Burns Weston.

Kant, I. (1781/2003*). Critique of Pure Reason*. Dover Publications.

BIBLIOGRAPHY

Kim, J. (2011). *Philosophy of Mind*. Third edition. Westview Press.

Kripke, S. (1980). *Naming and Necessity*. Harvard University Press.

Ladyman, J., Ross, D., Spurrett, D. & Collier, J. (2007). *Every Thing Must Go*. Oxford University Press.

Leibniz, G. W. (1714/2017). *Monadology*. Translated by J. Bennett. Freely available at https://www.earlymoderntexts.com/assets/pdfs/leibniz1714b.pdf

Levine, J. (1983). Materialism and Qualia: The Explanatory Gap. *Pacific Philosophical Quarterly*, 64: 354–361.

Mach, E. (1883/1942). *The Science of Mechanics*. Open Court.

McDonough, J. K. (2014). Leibniz's Philosophy of Physics. In *The Stanford Encyclopedia of Philosophy (Spring 2014 edition)*, E. N. Zalta (ed.). https://plato.stanford.edu/archives/spr2014/entries/leibniz-physics/

McGinn, C. (1989). Can We Solve the Mind-Body Problem? *Mind, New Series*, 98(391): 349–366.

McGinn, C. (2006). Hard Questions: Comments on Galen Strawson. *Journal of Consciousness Studies*, 13(10–11): 90–99.

McLaughlin, B. P. (2001). In Defence of New Wave Materialism: A Response to Horgan and Tienson. In *Physicalism and Its Discontents*, C. Gillett & B. Loewer (eds.). Cambridge University Press.

Miller, G. (2018). Can Subjects Be Proper Parts of Subjects? The De-Combination Problem. *Ratio*, 31(2): 137–154.

Montero, B. (2006). Physicalism in an Infinitely Decomposable World. *Erkenntnis*, 64(2): 177–191.

Mørch, H. H. (2014). Panpsychism and Causation: A New Argument and a Solution to the Combination Problem. Doctoral dissertation, University of Oslo.

Mørch, H. H. (2018). Is the Integrated Information Theory of Consciousness Compatible with Russellian Panpsychism? *Erkenntnis*, online publication.

Nagasawa, Y. & Wager, K. (2016). Panpsychism and Priority Cosmopsychism In *Panpsychism*, G. Brüntrup & L. Jaskolla (eds.). Oxford University Press.

Oizumi, M., Albantakis, L. &Tononi, G. (2014). From the Phenomenology to the Mechanisms of Consciousness: Integrated Information Theory 3.0. *PLoS Comput Biol* 10(5). https://doi.org/10.1371/journal.pcbi.1003588.

Peirce, C. S. (1866/1982). Lowell Lecture IX. In *Writings of Charles S. Peirce: A Chronological Edition*, M. H. Fisch (ed.). Indiana University Press.

Pinker, S. (2007). The Brain: The Mystery of Consciousness. *Time magazine*. Available online at http://content.time.com/time/magazine/article/0,9171,1580394,00.html.

Prior, E., Pargetter, R. & Jackson, F. (1982). Three theses about dispositions. *American Philosophical Quarterly*, 19 3): 251–257.

Putnam, H. (1975). The Meaning of "Meaning". *In Mind, Language, and Reality*, H. Putnam (ed.). Cambridge University Press.

Pylkkänen, P. T. I. (2007). *Mind, Matter and the Implicate Order*. Springer.

Ramsey, W. (2013). Eliminative Materialism. In *The Stanford Encyclopedia of Philosophy (Winter 2016 edition)*, E. N. Zalta (ed.). https://plato.stanford.edu/entries/materialism-eliminative/.

Robinson, H. (2017). Dualism. In *The Stanford Encyclopedia of Philosophy (Fall 2017 edition)*, E. N. Zalta (ed.). https://plato.stanford.edu/archives/fall2017/entries/dualism/.

Rosenberg, G. (2004). *A Place for Consciousness*. Oxford University Press.

BIBLIOGRAPHY

Rosenberg, G. (2016). Land Ho? We Are Close to a Synoptic Understanding of Consciousness In *Panpsychism*, G. Brüntrup & L. Jaskolla (eds.). Oxford University Press.

Russell, B. (1912). *Problems of Philosophy*. Home University Library.

Russell, B. (1927). *The Analysis of Matter*. Routledge.

Schaffer, J. (2003). Is There a Fundamental Level? *Noûs*, 37(3): 498–517.

Schaffer, J. (2010). Monism: The Priority of the Whole. *Philosophical Review,* 119(1): 31–76.

Seager, W. (1995). Consciousness, Information, and Panpsychism. *Journal of Consciousness Studies*, 2(3): 272–288.

Seager, W. (2006). The 'Intrinsic Nature' Argument for Panpsychism. *Journal of Consciousness Studies*, 13(10–11): 129–145.

Seager, W. (2010). Panpsychism, Aggregation and Combinatorial Infusion. *Mind and Matter* 8(2): 167–184.

Seager, W. (2016). Panpsychist Infusion. In *Panpsychism*, G. Brüntrup & L. Jaskolla (eds.). Oxford University Press.

Seager, W. (2020, ed.). *The Routledge Handbook of Panpsychism*. Oxford University Press.

Shani, I. (2015). Cosmopsychism: A Holistic Approach to the Metaphysics of Experience. *Philosophical Papers,* 44(3): 389–437.

Shani, I. & Keppler, J. (2018). Beyond Combination: How Cosmic Consciousness Grounds Ordinary Experience. *Journal of the American Philosophical Association*, 4(3): 390–410.

Sider, T. (2001). Maximality and Intrinsic Properties. *Philosophy and Phenomenological Research*, 63: 357–364.

Sider, T. (2003). Maximality and microphysical supervenience. *Philosophy and Phenomenological Research*, 66: 139–149.

Skrbina, D. (2011). Mind Space: toward a solution to the combination problem. In *The Mental as Fundamental: New Perspectives on Panpsychism*, M. Blamauer (ed.). De Bruyer.

Skrbina, D. (2017). *Panpsychism in the West*. Revised edition. MIT Press.

Sprigge, T. L. S. & Montefiore, A. (1971). Final Causes. *Proceedings of the Aristotelian Society*, 45 (Suppl.): 149–192.

Stoljar, D. (2001). Two Conceptions of the Physical. *Philosophical and Phenomenological Research*, 62(2): 253–281.

Strawson, G. (2006a). Realistic Materialism: Why Physicalism Entails Panpsychism. *Journal of Consciousness Studies*, 13(10–11): 3–31.

Strawson, G. (2006b). Panpsychism? Replies to Commentators and a Celebration of Descartes. *Journal of Consciousness Studies*, 13(10–11): 184–280.

Strawson, G. (2016). Mind and Being: The Primacy of Panpsychism. In *Panpsychism*, G. Brüntrup & L. Jaskolla (eds.). Oxford University Press.

Telakivi, P. (2020). Extending the Extended Mind: From Cognition to Consciousness.

Tononi, G. (2004). An Information Integration Theory of Consciousness. *BMC Neuroscience*, 5(42). Freely accessible at https://www.ncbi.nlm.nih.gov/pmc/articles/PMC543470/.

Turausky, K. (unpublished). Picturing Panpsychism: New Approaches to the Combination Problem. Available at academia.edu: https://bit.ly/2Qn7lIe.

INDEX

access consciousness 18
aggregative property 65
Albahari, M. 59
argument from intrinsic natures 37–42
argument from simplicity 41

Baars, B. 103
Block, N. 17–18
Broad, C. D. 27n17
Brüntrup, G. 27, 29n19, 39

Callicott, J. B. 15n5
causal nexus 97–98, 104–105
    completed 101
Cerullo, M. 18
Chalmers, D. 13, 26, 31–36, 45, 49, 54–55, 58–59, 60–61, 66–67, 75–77, 81, 111
Churchland, P. 18n8
co-consciousness 71, 74
cognitive consciousness 18 See also access consciousness
combination problem 53-61
conceivability argument 31–36
consciousness constraint 19, 42, 109
Coleman, S. 25n14, 50, 51n40, 59, 79
cosmophenomenal 52 See also cosmopsychism
cosmopsychism 51–52, 84–95, 110–111
    and the quality combination problem 94–95
    and the structural mismatch problem 95
    and the subject-summing problem 94

deBroglie-Bohm interpretation of quantum mechanics 90
decombination problem 84–86, 93–95
Dennett, D. 18
derivation problem See decombination problem
direct reference thesis 33–34
dualism
    substance 29, 44
    property 44

effective properties 97–98, 104–105
    primitive 101
emergence 26–30
    weak and strong 26, 62–63
    superstrong 27
    radical 27–28
epiphenomenalism 29, 63

121

PANPSYCHISM AND THE COMBINATION PROBLEM

existence monism 85
explanatory gap 13
extended mind 76n52
extrinsic nature 36–42
Eysenck, M. 78
Feigl, H. 51
Flanagan, O. 50
fundamentality 23–25
fundamental tone 80–81, 91, 94, 104–105, 107, 110–111

global workspace theory 103
Goff, P. 19–20, 21–22, 34–35, 41, 49–50, 52, 55–57, 59, 68, 73–76, 78, 81–82, 86–88, 93
grain problem 54 See also structural mismatch problem
grounding
    by analysis 23–25, 55–57, 84
    by subsumption 84
    partial 89–90

hard problem of consciousness 13

idealism 111–112
infusionism 47, 63–72
    and the perspective objection 70–71
    and the quality combination problem 70–71
    and the structural mismatch problem 71
    and the subject-summing problem 68–69
integrated information theory 81–83, 103

intrinsic nature 36–42

Jackson, F. 26n16, 69n49
James, W. 50n38, 53–54

Kant, I. 39n29
Keppler, J. 52, 88–95, 110
Kripke, S. 33–34

Ladyman, J. 38, 109
Leibniz, G. W. 16, 39n29
Levine, J. 13
logical positivism 16

Mach, E. 51
maximal property 64–65
McGinn, C. 50n38
McLaughlin, B. 35
Miller, G. 85
mind-body problem 14
mind dust 53
monadology 46
Montero, B. 25n14, 51n40
mysterianism 12, 50, 70, 72, 76
Mørch, H. H. 63, 72n50, 81–83

Nagasawa, Y. 51n40, 52, 84–86, 93
Nagel, T. 12
natural individual 101, 103–105
Nietzsche, F. 16
non-cognitive consciousness 18
    See also phenomenal consciousness

ontic structural realism 109

INDEX

palette problem 54 *See also* quality combination problem
  and phenomenal bonding 78–80
panpsychism 14–17, 43–52
  constitutive and non-constitutive 44–48
  diachronic emergent 47
  identity 46–47, 63
  synchronic emergent 45–46, 62–63
panprotopsychism 49–51
panqualityism 50–51
Peirce, C. S. 18
perspective objection 59
  and cosmopsychism 86, 95
  and infusionism 70–71
  and the theory of natural individuals 105–106
phenomenal bonding 73–83
  and the quality combination problem 76–81
  and the structural mismatch problem 81–83
  and the subject-summing problem 74–76
phenomenal consciousness 17–20
physical
  narrow and broad 36–37
  t-physical and o-physical 36
physicalism 21–23
  emergent 12, 25–30, 108
Pinker, S. 50n39
Plato 16
potentiality filters 96–97
priority monism 51–52
process ontology 112

protophenomenal 22, 49 *See also* panprotopsychism
Putnam, H. 34
Pylkkänen, P. 90n58

qualia 18–19, 40
quality combination problem 54, 57–60
  and cosmopsychism 94–95
  and infusionism 70–71
  and phenomenal bonding 76–81
  and the theory of natural individuals 104–105
quantum entanglement 66–67
quantum holism 66–67
quiddity 38, 49–50, 58n45

receptive connection 101–102 *See also* causal nexus
receptive property 97–98, 104–105
  primitive 100
revelation 35
Rosenberg, G. 73, 96–107, 110, 112
Russell, B. 37

Schaffer, J. 51–52, 86
Schopenhauer, A. 16
Seager, W. 38n26, 47, 53, 63–69, 71
Shani, I. 52, 59, 84, 88–95, 110
Sider, T. 64–65
Skrbina, D. 15n5, 16n6, 30, 61, 76n52
smallism 25n14, 51–52, 87–88
Spinoza, B. 16
stochastic electrodynamics 90–95
Stoljar, D. 36

Strawson, G. 19, 21–22, 27–28, 35, 41, 44, 79
structural mismatch problem 54, 60–61
    and cosmopsychism 95
    and infusionism 71
    and phenomenal bonding 81–83
    and the theory of natural individuals 106–107
subject-summing problem 54, 55–57
    and cosmopsychism 94–95
    and infusionism 68–69
    and phenomenal bonding 74–76
    and the theory of natural individuals 103–104
synoptic pyramid of consciousness 103

Telakivi, P. 76n52
theory of causal significance 96–97
theory of natural individuals 96–107, 110–111
    and the quality combination problem 104–105
    and the structural mismatch problem 106–107
    and the subject-summing problem 103–104
Tononi, G. 81–83, 103
Turausky, K. 80–81, 91, 94, 104–105, 107
two-dimensional semantics 33–34

Wager, K. 52, 84–86, 93

zero-point field 90–95
zombies 36–37, 57, 69, 76

www.ingramcontent.com/pod-product-compliance
Lightning Source LLC
Chambersburg PA
CBHW021114080526
44587CB00010B/518